# Tailoring the Green Suit

# Tailoring the Green Suit

## Empowering Yourself for an Executive Career in the New Green Economy

Dan Smolen

authorHOUSE®

AuthorHouse™
1663 Liberty Drive
Bloomington, IN 47403
www.authorhouse.com
Phone: 1-800-839-8640

© 2011 Dan Smolen. All rights reserved.

No part of this book may be reproduced, stored in a retrieval system, or transmitted by any means without the written permission of the author.

First published by AuthorHouse 3/9/2011

ISBN: 978-1-4490-5979-8 (sc)
ISBN: 978-1-4490-5981-1 (e)
ISBN: 978-1-4490-5980-4 (hc)

Library of Congress Control Number: 2010903633

Printed in the United States of America

This book is printed on acid-free paper.

Two percent of the author's revenue from this book will be donated to Friends of the Rappahannock, a non-governmental organization providing environmentally-responsible civic planning and public education resources to Virginia's historic Rappahannock River region. Learn more at: www.riverfriends.org.

# Dedication

To the two people who made me possible: Arnie Smolen, who passed on to me the dominant serial-entrepreneur gene and inspires me each and every day by living his life with honesty, personal integrity, and passion. *What a mensch!* And Riva Smolen, who instilled in me a love of nature and life's simplest pleasures and reminds me that family is indeed everything. Love you both!

*Tikkun Olam*
(Heal the world.)

# Contents

Dedication .................................................................................. v

Preface ..................................................................................... xi

Introduction:
 The Green Paradigm Shift ................................................ xiii
 – The Convergence ........................................................ xiv
 – The Green Suits ......................................................... xvii
 – Millennials—The Quantum Force in the New Green
  Economy ................................................................. xviii

Chapter 1:
 Empowerment Starts With the Thread—Defining a Green
 Business Executive Job ........................................................ 1
 – The Green Business Executive Universe ........................ 3
 – Obvious Green Business Executive Jobs ........................ 6
 – Not-So-Obvious Green Business Executive Jobs ............ 9
 – History ...................................................................... 10
 – Energy ....................................................................... 13
 – Green Jobs, Red-Hot Controversy .............................. 17
 – Corporate Social Responsibility .................................. 18

Chapter 2:
 Gather "Fabric" of Your Green Business Executive Career—
 Education and Training ...................................................... 23
 – Gather and Analyze Information ................................. 24
 – Acquire Knowledge and Experience ............................ 26
 – Gain Accreditation .................................................... 28
 – Politics vs. Green Business Executive Career Education
  and Training .............................................................. 32

Chapter 3:
Taking Measure—Seeking Out, Landing, and Creating Your
Green Business Executive Job ................................................................35
- Establish Your Value Proposition ..............................................35
- Write or Revise Your Résumé ....................................................36
- Peruse the Job Boards ................................................................42
- Contact Companies, Strategically ..............................................42
- Build Your Network ..................................................................43
- Consider Blogging .................................................................... 44
- Engage with Executive Recruiters ..............................................45
- Prepare for Job Interviews ........................................................ 46
- Establish an Interview Strategy ..................................................47
- Create Your Own Green Business Executive Job ................ 48

Chapter 4:
Pressing The Green Suit's Corporate Culture ............................... 51
- Things You Can Do to Establish Corporate Greenness ........ 51
- Create Your Own Advisory Board ............................................55
- Get on the Fast Track to Understanding Regulation ............56
- From the Bottom Up: Gain Staff Input on Sustainability ....56

Chapter 5:
If the Suit Fits … WEAR IT! ......................................................59
- Perfect Your Three-Floor Elevator Pitch ...............................59
- Speak at Professional Meetings and Conferences ..................61
- Write Columns and Opinion Editorials for Business
  Publications ............................................................................62
- Mentor the Green Suits of the Future ....................................63
- Promote Green Business Executive Job Fairs ......................63
- Walk the Walk ................................................................... 64

Chapter 6:
Not Cut Out for Corporate Life? Fashion Yourself the Green-
Suited Entrepreneur ................................................................... 71
- The Pioneering Green Manufacturer .....................................72
- The Green Marketer ................................................................72
- The Green Consultant/Collaborator ......................................74
- The Green Designer ...............................................................74

- The Virtual Assistant ............................................................. 75
- The "Climate Superhero" Motivator ..................................... 76

Conclusion:
Properly Attired, Our Best Days Lie Ahead! .............................. 77

Bibliography ............................................................................... 83

Acknowledgments ...................................................................... 97

Index ........................................................................................ 101

About the Author ..................................................................... 111

# Preface

*Tailoring the Green Suit* is about the *process* of developing a successful executive career in the new green economy. It is a career development book for U.S. business executives seeking employment in green business. This book is for business executives who are predisposed to careers in renewable energy, resource sustainability, and corporate social responsibility, or executives who are interested in joining fast-growing, potentially lucrative green or sustainable industries. These industries may offer the greatest number and variety of future career opportunities. The potential universe of U.S. green business executives may be as high as *sixty-eight million people*.

This book provides several detailed steps executives may take to develop and sustain satisfying careers in the field. These steps include: determining what a green business executive job is; acquiring green business executive career education and training; seeking out and landing a green business executive job; fostering a green business corporate culture; being a public advocate for green business executive careers; and considering a green business entrepreneurial career path. After reading this book, I hope you will have at your disposal the tools you need to begin a long and successful executive career in green business.

Green business executives are trailblazers and industry ambassadors. As leaders, we must strive to keep the bar high and work toward building a strong and sustainable business, together.

The informational content of this book is derived from several sources: primary research from interviews; secondary research such as recent business studies, news reports, and corporate media releases; and insight I have gathered as an executive recruiter, marketer, entrepreneur, public policy activist, and committed environmentalist.

There are so many people I must thank for their guidance in

helping make this book possible. I have listed their names in the acknowledgment section at the end. But there are a few people who deserve a special shout-out, right up front:

Lawrence Mayers is my mentor. After a successful and lucrative fifty-plus-year career in marketing and executive recruiting, Lawrence remains very much in the game; he is by far my sharpest, most knowledgeable resource, and my most enthusiastic business partner. This book would never have gone to print without Lawrence's sage advice, encouragement, and good humor.

Stuart Katz of Elm City Communications and I have been the closest of friends since kindergarten. I sought and received his unvarnished feedback of the manuscript and leveraged his knowledge and experience as a successful start-up entrepreneur, marketing communications and electronic-media expert, and well-respected adjunct professor of corporate communications, to ensure that this book is interesting, relevant, and immediately useful.

Last, the love of my life, my wife Marsha, who encouraged me throughout the entire book-writing process, provided spot-on book-writing and design advice, and served as my most trusted sounding board. And our daughter Daryn—a member of "Generation Z" and the world's best kid—whose enthusiasm for life and thoughtful questions about our planet's future motivated me to create an interesting and valuable career-development resource. *Daddy owes you lots of hugs and kisses!*

To the aspiring green business executives reading this book, I say thank you and enjoy the ride: *our best days lie ahead!*

> – Dan Smolen
> Stafford, Virginia
> December 2009

# Introduction:
## The Green Paradigm Shift

We bear witness to a green paradigm shift, one so large and dramatic that it is changing the way we live and work. Most certainly, it will change how management executives embark on their careers.

If a "paradigm shift" is the transformation of public consciousness due to the acceptance of new ideas previously thought impossible or unacceptable, then the "green paradigm shift" is the public's sudden recognition that renewable energy, conservation and resource-sustainability, and corporate social responsibility are transforming how we:

- Power our homes, schools, and factories;
- Commute to work;
- Build wealth;
- Invent and market new technologies;
- Relate to and support local and global communities, and;
- Mitigate global warming.

Further, the green paradigm shift has ushered in the age of "the triple bottom line." The term was coined in 1994 by global sustainability expert John Elkington, to add social and environmental values to a company's traditional economic measures. The triple bottom line is often referred to as "The Three Ps." They are as follows: People, Planet, Profit.

## The Convergence

A multitude of factors have converged to usher in the green paradigm shift.

- Concerns that the world's oil reserves are drying up combined with a record-high dependency on foreign oil have caused corporations and consumers to bolster calls for the exploration and development of clean and renewable energy from wind, solar, geothermal, and biomass.

- Titans of industry, who perhaps five years ago would have scoffed at a renewable energy future, are among its most unlikely champions; chief among the former naysayers is T. Boone Pickens, whose *Pickens Plan* for renewable energy has led the zeitgeist.

- Several large industrial companies, once considered prime polluters and abusers of the world's natural resources, are leading the corporate green movement. Among them are: IBM, Wal-Mart, AT&T, Dow Chemical, and Cisco Systems.

- Renewable energy, sustainability, and corporate social responsibility are no longer solely dominated by left-leaning politicians and grassroots activists. Mainstream religious groups, middle-American civic organizations, and enterprises of all sizes are embracing sustainability. From sole proprietorships to the Fortune 500, all kinds of businesses are turning green. And with "Ecomagination," "Green is Universal," and other green-themed campaigns, GE and its many divisions are demonstrating a thorough commitment to the environment.

- Savvy marketers and manufacturers are growing ever mindful of greenwashing concerns or the deceptive practice of extending dubious green claims. And some are going to great lengths to provide consumers a fully transparent view of their growing, manufacturing, packaging, marketing, and distribution processes. For instance:

- In 2009, consumer packaged goods manufacturer S.C. Johnson sought to increase transparency by voluntarily disclosing the use of fragrances, dyes, and preservatives in its products;

- Continental Clothing brought transparency to the fore by listing all of the processes it follows to manufacture "earth positive" clothing. These include: using low-impact farming and carbon-neutral manufacturing facilities, minimizing water usage, and following fair trade and employment practices;

- And Stonyfield Farm has launched the ClimateCounts.org Web site to hold it and other companies accountable for their impact on global warming. Company CEO Gary Hirschberg believes that progressive companies will some day gain considerable competitive advantages by listing third-party verified Life Cycle Assessments (LCAs) of their own products' impact on the environment.

- Companies that once scoffed at allowing staff to tele-work are now providing the option as a means of boosting productivity and retaining top executive talent. Coincidentally, the exurban population migration of the 1980s to 2000s appears to be ebbing. More workers are choosing to live closer to inner cities and sustainability-focused companies are encouraging their employees to use mass transit by providing full or partial fair subsidies; defense contractor SAIC provides employees who participate in its carpool incentive program cash reimbursements of up to $120 per month. And some companies, such as renewable energy company First Wind, are leaving suburbia for locations within city limits to attract more employees who use mass transit.

- Communities are running out of landfill capacity across the U.S. Large cities such as Philadelphia and San Francisco have exceeded their landfill capacity limits, while for the last thirty years the city of New York has trucked much of its solid waste hundreds of miles south to landfills such as the massive facility in King George, Virginia. And considering the long-term toxicity of landfill waste, communities such as Montgomery County, Maryland, and Cape May, New Jersey, have imposed strict recycling measures on homeowners and businesses. Throughout Northern Virginia, municipal recycling centers have put special procedures in place for the proper disposal of refuse considered too toxic for general collection, such as: oil-based and latex paints, industrial cleaners and solvents, waste motor oil and automotive fluids, pesticides, and other lawn and garden chemistry.

- Smart-grid technologies—devices that communicate directly with electrical appliances so that those appliances draw electrical current more efficiently—are about to revolutionize how we power our homes, businesses, and motor vehicles. The U.S. military has ordered that any new construction or renovations to existing installations employ so-called smart energy meters.

- Businesses and consumers wanting to *go green* are replacing millions of incandescent light bulbs with compact fluorescent lights (CFLs). U.S. federal law has mandated the phase out of incandescent lighting starting in 2012. Wal-Mart already leads worldwide retail sales of these new CFLs.

- Company supply chains are becoming green. Businesses are developing and implementing best practices to ensure that the ways their products are grown, built, packaged, shipped, and delivered yield the smallest carbon footprint.

- The need for clean water is finally being taken seriously as its availability across the globe decreases. Savvy investors consider water a tradable commodity, and some of them think water is the next crude oil. As a result, new water recycling and reclamation technologies and practices are being developed.

- One generational cohort, known as "Generation Y" or "the Millennials," has entered the workforce en masse, and they are changing how executives lead the workplace. This generation has already tilted business mindsets in the direction of sustainability and corporate social responsibility.

- And last, many corporate managers and entrepreneurs are realizing that businesses embracing green practices will now benefit greatly through improved revenue generation, market share, and return on investment (ROI). The bottom line on the triple bottom line: corporations late to the green gate will be left in the proverbial dust.

## The Green Suits

This book does not survey the wider green jobs array, nor is it a how-to book for landing so-called green collar jobs. Rather, this book addresses the segment of the labor pool that has been greatly overlooked in the green jobs discussion: management executives who are already in—or will some day be a part of—the new green economy's workforce.

I call these men and women The Green Suits. They are ambitious business executives who are in, or wish to enter, the renewable energy and conservation sectors. They are executives looking to turn their conventional companies and market verticals green. *And they are hell bent on changing the world.*

Whether they have earned fresh bachelors, masters, or doctoral degrees or have been part of the executive ranks for the past twenty-five-plus years, many business executives will be drawn into green business by the prospects of career success and monetary reward. Many executives will also be guided by their own strong sense of social conscience and will seek management executive employment opportunities in green business so that they may *do well* and *do right*, making the world a better place.

No aspect of business will be more impacted by the new green economy than human capital. Executives who acquire current green business information and knowledge and who quickly become green leaders in their companies and organizations will enjoy far greater career success and satisfaction than those who are late to the green gate.

## Millennials—The Quantum Force in the New Green Economy

In their groundbreaking book, *Millennial Makeover*, authors Mike Hais and Morley Winograd write about the Millennials (or Generation Y). They argue that this formidable generational cohort—raised on Barney the purple dinosaur and adult-organized and supervised group play—will have a huge impact on society, public policy, and world economics. The environmentally friendly Millennials are an even larger demographic cohort than the Baby Boomer Generation. Where Millennial's Baby Boomer parents were aptly labeled in the first-person singular narrative as the "Me" Generation, Millennials are defined by (their) collaborative, shared experiences: they are the "We" Generation. As such, Millennials are truly passionate about working in collaboration with other likeminded people to solve the world's vexing environmental and social ills. And given their sheer numbers, Millennials are indeed well-placed to drive explosive growth and innovation in the new green economy. What is more, Millennials will change how society views and processes executive work, how such work will be compensated, and where the work will be done; Millennials already are a potent force advocating virtual office work (telecommuting).

But perhaps of greatest importance, Millennials will recast business management executives as agents for a better, more sustainable world through ethical, socially responsible commerce.

Over the next twenty to thirty years, the workforces of the world's economies will turn decidedly green. And while the planet will be led by the Millennial-aged executives into this new green business world, hired talent will still need to be well-informed and educated in the areas of renewable energy, conservation, sustainability, and corporate social responsibility. In military parlance, going green is mission critical.

The transformation we are about to experience will be breathtaking. The definition of green companies or green business executives— The Green Suits—will develop and evolve on a daily basis. Blazing innovations in the areas of renewable energy production, smart grid technology, and energy conservation will happen so quickly that our understanding of the new green economy will require continued and frequent calibration. It won't be enough for the talented, ambitious, green-focused executive to attend industry gatherings every once in a while. Learning will need to become part of The Green Suits' daily regimen, requiring a near constant flow of the latest news, information, and knowledge to retain their status as green business thought leaders. But remaining well-trained and educated in the green business world need not be onerous. The manner in which such information and knowledge is imparted will be ever-evolving, and the pace of its delivery will be equally mind-blowing.

Building a solid, successful business career is a lot like tailoring a business suit: the garment must balance form (fashion) and function (utility). And it enables the wearer, perhaps facing a room full of formidable and reliably skeptical senior business executives, to project an appropriate air of confidence and professionalism.

One of the difficulties of getting into a work-in-progress field like green business is that there is very little information available to help guide a pioneering careerist. When I graduated from college in the early 1980s, I chuckled at the suggestion posed by the "Jimmy Early" character in the Broadway show *Dreamgirls* to "fake your way to the top." And absent work experience and work-related training and education, some in my generation took that suggestion quite literally. But in today's economy—and especially in the new green business world—that won't fly. One's career success *will* be tied to transparency. *No faking will be tolerated.*

Being The Green Suit is no different. It will take great forethought, access to quality material, thought leadership, a penchant for ideation and collaboration with other like-minded executives, fire-in-the-belly enthusiasm and ambition, and time to fashion a winning career path. Think of this book as the tailor, helping you achieve a custom fit in your green business executive career.

Whether you are an experienced business executive looking to pivot into a green business career or a fresh-out-of-school entry-level executive, know this: your future can be bright green, totally rewarding, and fun.

Now, let's gather the fabric of your future and lay out the step-by-step tailoring plan for you to become The Green Suit.

# Chapter 1:
## Empowerment Starts With the Thread— Defining a Green Business Executive Job

Your empowerment begins by taking on the challenge that vexes many of us already in the green business space: defining a green business executive job.

Does a green job have to be directly connected with the green energy industry? Does a green job have to be expressly sustainability focused?

Perhaps so. Then again, perhaps not.

The term "green jobs" has so permeated our daily conversations that few can agree what it actually means. And, in light of 2009's controversial resignation of White House green jobs czar Van Jones, the green jobs issue has become suffused with partisan political rhetoric.

Many believe the term "green jobs" applies primarily to "green-collar jobs," or what some critics call "blue-collar jobs turned green." While the collar reference may be relevant for a wide swath of the American workforce, it doesn't apply to the millions of business management executives interested in becoming green.

So, what are some of the current working-definitions of green jobs? Spooled up for your consideration are these examples:

In October 2008, the United Nations Environment Programme (UNEP) ventured into the fray with this definition:

> [We] define green jobs as work in agricultural, manufacturing, research and development, administrative, and services activities that contribute

> substantially to preserving or restoring environmental quality. Specifically, but not exclusively, this includes jobs that help protect ecosystems and biodiversity; reduce energy, materials, and water consumption through high efficiency strategies; de-carbonize the economy; and minimize or altogether avoid generation of all forms of waste or pollution.

Next, David Foster, the executive director of the BlueGreen Alliance, chimes in:

> A green job is a blue-collar job done for a green purpose.

Interesting, and succinct for sure, but Foster's definition completely ignores the green business executive ranks, The Green Suits.

Tracy Crawford, the founding partner of Technical Green, LLC, a nationally recognized sustainability-focused technology recruitment advertising and social media firm, adds that key to any green job is that "[it] doesn't involve outsourcing to countries with poor environmental records" but does promote "working for a better world."

In June 2009, green marketing advisor and noted speaker Jane Tabachnick commenced a green jobs summit in New York by asking panelists, "What is the definition of a green job?" Summarized from Tabachnick's *EnvironmentalLeader.com* blog post:

> While the panelists present bristled at the terms "green" and "green jobs," Tabachnick's group did identify some key attributes that previous definitions left out. For instance: a green job could be one that has as its sole purpose a direct positive impact on the environment; or, a green job could be a job—such as an accountant—at a green company.

Actually, Tabachnick and her panel show how difficult it is to create an accurate and succinct green job definition. And many are left asking: is a green job solely focused on inherently environmental work, or is a green job *any job* at a green-focused company or a company committed to sustainability and corporate social responsibility?

To add some challenge to the tailoring, consider the confusion over how many green jobs—*green business executive jobs*—there are already and how many there may be five, ten, or twenty years down the line. For sure, many millions of green jobs will be created, but no one can reliably offer more than a ballpark estimate.

All this confusion and hairsplitting reminds me of the old joke about a gathering of rabbis. Ask six of them what a green job is and they'll come back with seven answers.

I propose that the term "green business executive job" describes executive and managerial employment in any *obvious* market segment (e.g., renewable energy, green building, environmental services, sustainable forestry) or *not-so-obvious* market segment (e.g., financial services, telecommunications, consumer product manufacturing) that:

- Serves to improve the company's triple bottom line;

- Extends the acceptance of, and participation in, carbon footprint reduction, recycling and conservation, renewable energy usage, mass transit commuting, virtual office work (telecommuting), and other related initiatives;

- Encourages corporate social responsibility through skill-based volunteerism and other practices;

- Promotes corporate transparency as it pertains to manufacturing, marketing, distribution, and sales of company products and services, and;

- Supports continued company-wide green business training and education.

## The Green Business Executive Universe

Many of us will, for some time to come, remain at odds over what constitutes a green job. However, there is little disagreement that the green job market will be huge. And a segment of the green workforce—

The Green Business Executive ranks—will be quite formidable in its own right. Based on U.S. government data and market research related to the green interests of American consumers, I have established a credible estimate of the Green Business Executive universe.

- First, using the U.S. Census Bureau's 2006 American Community Survey, I tallied approximately 84.7 million white-collar workers employed in management, professional, sales, and office-related assignments.

- Second, I overlaid findings from a 2008 study by Virginia-based consumer market research firm Rockbridge Associates, which indicated that approximately 80 percent of the U.S. population has positive opinions of green products and companies that, to some degree, practice sustainability and corporate social responsibility. I call these consumers Green Favorable. Preferences at home are likely to be reflected as preferences at work, thus 80 percent of the 84.7 million white-collar universe—or 67.8 million—are Green Favorable business executives.

- The Rockbridge Associates study also indicated that 60 percent of consumers are motivated by green and sustainable ideals. Thus, within the 84.7 million white-collar workforce are estimated to be 50.8 million of what I call Green Motivated. This cohort of executives may, if given the choice, purchase a green product or service over ones that are not, even if the green choice costs more than the non-green choice.

- Within the Green Motivated cohort are Green Practicing types. I have not been able to find reliable data to represent a Green Practicing universe, thus I corralled the top three deciles (the top 30 percent) of the Green Motivated group to set an estimate of 15.2 million. Green Practicing types are purpose-driven, and act well beyond green product or services purchases to demonstrate their greenness. They are knowledgeable about the effects of global warming, and they are well-read on the subjects of renewable energy, sustainability, and corporate social responsibility practices. Greenness defines them.

As defined:

| Detail | (millions) | |
|---|---|---|
| Total estimated U.S. population (2006 American Community Survey) | 299.3 | |
| - Workforce-management/professionals (16%) | 48.0 | |
| - Workforce-sales and office positions (12.3%) | 36.7 | |
| Sub-Total | 84.7 | |
| Green Favorable (80% of sub-total) | 67.8 | |
| Green Motivated (60% of sub-total) | 50.8 | |
| Green Practicing (30% of Green Motivated) | 15.2 | |
| Unique Cohorts | | |
| Green Practicing (15.2) | | 15.2 million |
| Green Motivated (50.8 less 15.2) | | 35.6 million |
| Green Favorable (67.8 less 15.2 less 35.6) | | 17.0 million |
| **Total Estimated U.S. Green Business Executives** | | **67.8 million** |

Here is a graphic representation of the quite formidable 67.8 million person universe of U.S. Green Business Executives:

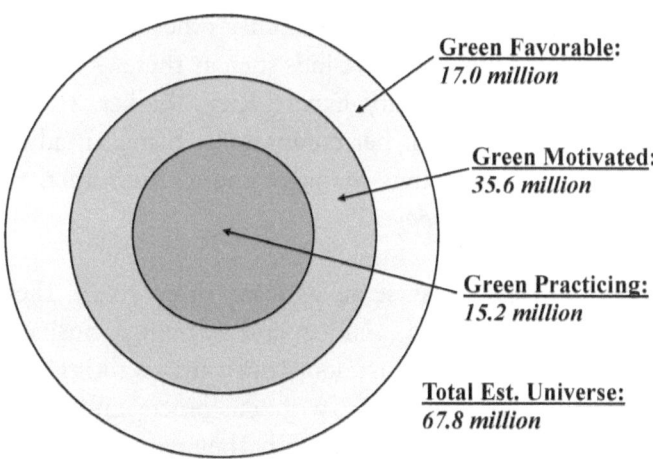

In the near term we must be patient. While the potential universe of green business executives is large, for the immediate future the green business executive job concept will remain a bit hazy. Given that no one truly knows what innovations lie ahead, staying open-minded and creative about what a green business executive job is or could be remains our best course of action. For now, let us accept that each and every green job definition swirling around boardrooms, water coolers, cable news shows, college lecture halls, and business-related social communities has validity.

Here is where we keep the thread from unraveling. For the sake of organization, let us divide the business executive employment opportunities into two groups: Obvious Green Business Executive Jobs and Not-So-Obvious Green Business Executive Jobs.

## Obvious Green Business Executive Jobs

Let us consider the obvious: the executive level jobs that will most likely have a direct impact on the environment, or a company's environmental policy. According to an October 16, 2008 post by Fortune.com reporter Anna Vander Broek, several of them are also the most in demand six-figure salary green executive jobs.

Chief among the obvious green business executive jobs is sustainability officer (also known as chief sustainability officer; sustainability director; chief green officer; sustainability manager; environmental officer). The rapid rise of corporate sustainability has ratcheted up the demand for sustainability officers. And most of the major U.S. corporations now have jobs such as these.

According to sustainability expert Rich Walker, this executive is tasked with leading his or her company by being an advocate and educator, a visionary, a change manager and a cheerleader, and above all else, *a results-driven manager*.

> These officers must serve at least three roles: They must look inward, end-to-end driving business opportunity; they must look outward, walking the talk and communicating with customers and other stakeholders; and they must lead. They must articulate,

implement, and sustain the organization's vision of sustainability and provide visibility and transparency of that vision both internally and externally. And they must have both the charisma and compelling message for the organization to want to follow and recognize the benefits, both financial and environmental.

Steve Boston is the chief sustainability officer at global enterprise management software powerhouse CA (formerly Computer Associates). In his role, Boston nurtures CA's worldwide resources to balance maximum return on investment, ambitious carbon abatement, and corporate social responsibility—the triple bottom line. Since spring 2008, Boston has overseen a global process at CA that has yielded a remarkable 41 percent reduction in the company's carbon footprint.

With a career that has been entirely IT software space-focused and includes twenty successful and rewarding years at IBM, Boston joined CA to oversee the corporation's global operations strategy. But soon after arriving, his responsibilities were expanded to include the company's sustainability and corporate social responsibility oversight.

Boston is by training and temperament an accomplished problem solver. He says being the CSO of CA provides him with a "huge set of problem-solving opportunities" from making sure that CA conserves power and natural resources to managing "the societal piece." Boston describes his mission as "a strange mix: half business manager, half [sustainability evangelist]."

Other obvious green business executive jobs include:

- Environmental engineers, who help clients understand how to mitigate environmental impacts, from reducing pollution to reducing carbon footprints and preserving wildlife and native plant species;

- Environmental attorneys, who may represent corporations or non-profit organizations. At corporations, they provide counsel to comply with federal, state, and local environmental regulation;

- Climatologists/environmental meteorologists, who study weather patterns and their effects on a corporation's industrial output. The work is especially important to companies in agribusiness, forestry, and other industries that leverage natural resources. Climatologists may also counsel management to apply environmental improvements that can mitigate wide scale climate change;

- Renewable energy managers, who oversee the generation and conservation of energy. Their work has significant implications for corporations, especially in the area of cost savings;

- Environmental specialists/scientists, who study air, food, and soil and look for pollutants that may cause health risk in humans, animal populations, and vegetation. Senior-level executive careers are often in government sector;

- And senior urban planners, who determine best practices for community land use. They balance the needs of neighborhoods, schools, and public facilities with commercial and industrial settings. Often they work in the public sector, but they may also work in the private sector. On Fastcompany.com, writer Anya Kamenetz describes urban planners as the "linchpin of the quest to lower America's carbon footprint."

One of the areas expected to benefit greatly from the green paradigm shift is Leadership in Energy and Design (LEED) construction. While not necessarily part of the executive ranks, professional-level opportunities will abound for LEED-certified architects, designers, electrical engineers, mechanical engineers, manufacturers, marketers, and other building trade professionals.

Other obvious green business executive jobs are being created in these fields: carbon offsetting; water recovery and recycling; wind turbine fabrication; geothermal cooling; and energy efficiency. And according to the UNEP study, several industries offer good or excellent green job development potential:

| Sector | Industry | Greening potential | Green jobs progress to date | Long-term green job potential |
|---|---|---|---|---|
| Energy | Renewable energy | Excellent | Good | Excellent |
| | Carbon capture and sequestration | Fair | None | Unknown |
| Industry | Steel | Good | Fair | Fair |
| | Aluminum | Good | Fair | Fair |
| | Cement | Fair | Fair | Fair |
| | Pulp and paper | Good | Fair | Good |
| | Recycling | Excellent | Good | Excellent |
| Transportation | Fuel-efficient cars | Fair to Good | Limited | Good |
| | Public transportation | Excellent | Limited | Excellent |
| | Rail | Excellent | Negative | Excellent |
| | Aviation | Limited | Limited | Limited |
| Building Trades | Green buildings | Excellent | Limited | Excellent |
| | Retrofitting | Excellent | Limited | Excellent |
| | Lighting | Excellent | Good | Excellent |
| | Efficient equipment and appliances | Excellent | Fair | Excellent |
| Agriculture | Small-scale sustainable farming | Excellent | Negative | Excellent |
| | Organic farming | Excellent | Limited | Good to Excellent |
| | Environmental services | Good | Limited | Unknown |
| Forestry | Reforestation | Good | Limited | Good |
| | Agroforestry | Good to Excellent | Limited | Good to Excellent |
| | Sustainable forestry management | Excellent | Good | Excellent |

SOURCE: *Green Jobs Towards Decent Work in a Sustainable, Low-Carbon World (UNEP/ILO/IOE/ITUC, Sept. 2008)*

# Not-So-Obvious Green Business Executive Jobs

There are green jobs all around us in companies that are not inherently green. Could a chief financial officer at a car company—a manufacturer of motor vehicles that emit exhaust containing $CO^2$ and other airborne pollutants—be The Green Suit? Given what you read previously, that few agree on a standard definition for a green job, I say: *why not?*

A conventional company could in fact be bright green. Consider Subaru of America (SOA). Unlike Toyota, Honda, Ford, GM, and Chrysler, SOA does not produce a single hybrid vehicle, and yet it is considered one of the most sustainability focused companies in the world. SOA's final assembly plant in Lafayette, Indiana reclaims 99 percent of its waste, and is situated by a large native bird reserve. And Ceres/Risk Metrics' December 2008 study entitled *Corporate Governance and Climate Change* considers these conventional consumer and technology companies as among the world's greenest: IBM; British supermarket chain Tesco plc; Dell; Intel; Johnson & Johnson; Nike; Wal-Mart; Applied Materials; and Coca-Cola.

Conceivably, any executive management role at any of the above companies—such as in manufacturing, sales, finance, client relations, marketing, information technology, operations, or supply chain—could be a Not-So-Obvious Green Job.

Abhi Vyas is a marketing manager for outdoor advertising media company MetroMedia Technologies in Dallas, Texas. When Vyas started working at MetroMedia several years ago, the company had no greenness about it; as their durable outdoor ads expired, the vinyl substrate material used to manufacture them was discarded in landfills, causing a big negative impact on the environment.

According to the research paper, *Environmental Impacts of Polyvinyl Chloride Building Materials: A Healthy Building Network Report* written and prepared by Joe Thornton, Ph.D., there are serious concerns related to vinyl disposal. First, vinyl products such as polyvinylchloride (PVC) may take centuries to decompose, demanding more landfill capacity than other waste; and vinyl is a known groundwater contaminate.

In 2006, Vyas "plunged into sustainability" when he joined the transformation team that deliberated on the best way to mitigate MetroMedia's landfill problem; the team developed a sustainability plan called *re:act* which MetroMedia's boardroom approved and quickly executed. Now, in partnership with fashion accessory company Vy and Elle, MetroMedia's expired outdoor ads, such as ones for Coca-Cola, are transformed into eye-catching ladies' handbags, wallets, and accessories such as iPod cases.

Vyas has gotten a lot of personal satisfaction contributing to his company's sustainability successes. Now he is a committed practitioner of sustainability who is eager to promote his company's earth-friendliness through social media and in particular, on MetroMedia's company blog.

## History

To understand the importance of green jobs, it helps to consider some historical perspective.

Over the past five hundred years, the world has experienced many seismic events—caused by war, famine, trade embargoes, technological advancements, exploration and exploitation, climate and geologic events, abrupt changes in fashion and taste—that have altered how people live, and most definitely how they work.

During its first two hundred years, America morphed from a colonial producer of agriculture and raw materials supporting the British mercantile class to an industrial powerhouse and producer of top-quality finished goods. America's forward thinking made it the marvel of the world.

While entrepreneurship and invention have always been important catalysts of the American economy, during the first half of the twentieth century the U.S. industrial model placed the greatest value on the biggest of the big industrial companies—U.S. Steel, American Telephone & Telegraph (AT&T), DuPont, and General Motors—that were also biggest consumers (and wasters) of water, energy, and other natural resources. Current-day irony aside, the saying, "what is good for General Motors is good for America," was a testament to the belief of many on Wall Street that larger meant better.

Meanwhile, the company man, characterized by columnist Ellen Goodman as the stalwart corporate careerist living the American Dream in suburbia, became an indelible symbol, the archetype of mid-twentieth century popular culture and hyper-consumerism.

In 1962, Rachel Carson's book *Silent Spring* helped start the environmental movement by raising concerns over pollution and the rampant use of pesticides. In the 1970s, such concern led to irrefutable evidence that some of the nation's biggest corporations such as General Electric had poisoned lakes and rivers with industrial runoff containing pollution and known carcinogens. The Hudson River, the source of drinking water for parts of New York State and a major commercial fishing area, was heavily poisoned by dioxin-laden industrial runoff. Many large companies spewed millions of metric tons in airborne waste from the unfiltered smokestacks of their coal-fired factories.

In July 1970, President Richard M. Nixon and the U.S. Congress established the Environmental Protection Agency (EPA). This new federal agency began applying unprecedented regulatory pressure on businesses to curb water and air pollution. The EPA forced strict environmental regulation across all industries, and some companies doled out billions of dollars to cover their regulatory fines.

Then in September 1970, in a *New York Times Magazine* piece entitled "The Social Responsibility of Business is to Increase its Profits," University of Chicago economist Milton Friedman wrote, "there is one and only one social responsibility of business—to use its resources and engage in activities designed to increase its profits so long as it stays within the rules of the game, which is to say, engages in open and free competition without deception or fraud."

Conglomerates, or large companies that spread financial risks across disparate divisions, such as paid parking companies, cable television outlets, and funeral and burial services, were the darlings of investors for much of the twentieth century. Scovill Manufacturing was an American corporation that took pride in its advertising claim as "the world's largest company."

*Today, how many people actually remember the brand name Scovill?*

But the 1980s ushered in a radical transformation of big business. A trend took hold in which the combined valuations of conglomerates' individual subsidiaries were almost always priced higher than the conglomerates as a whole. And what at the time seemed like a near daily event, many big holding companies were ripped apart by hostile takeovers. One of the most famous hostile takeovers in American history, Kohlberg Kravis Roberts' twenty-five billion dollar acquisition of RJR Nabisco in 1989, became the subject of Bryan Burrough's and John Helyar's best-selling book, *Barbarians at the Gate*, and led many corporate boardrooms to a state of bunker mentality.

This new trend single-handedly eviscerated the company man construct. Many of these old school careerists who often placed their loyalty to corporate management above personal interests were pink slipped. Adding insult to injury, some of them would discover that they had lost hundreds of thousands of dollars in 401k retirement savings that corporate management invested in worthless company securities.

Fabled corporate raiders, epitomized by the Gordon Gecko character in the movie *Wall Street*, cajoled stockholders to accept hostile takeovers, telling them that divestiture was in their best interests. But the downside of hostile takeovers would be felt immediately: loyal workers—the company men (and also company women)—became faceless, easily expendable, and highly disposable human capital units. The U.S. (and to some extent other industrialized nations) saw meaner, leaner, more profitable companies take shape.

Also in the 1980s, the industrialized world entered the Information Age. While founded in 1975, it was during the early 1980s that Federal Express (now FedEx) gained great popularity by making overnight package delivery between two faraway points the norm. Office fax machines became ubiquitous, allowing business communications that might have taken days by mail to be faxed in a matter of seconds. This saved corporations considerable time, money, and support staff expense. It was during the early 1980s that the personal computer went from office luxury to necessity.

Those employees lucky enough not to be downsized were retrained and motivated to become more productive on the job, which often meant more career specialization and longer hours at work. The pejorative term "type A personality" was foisted upon high achievers who chose evening hours and weekends at the office over marriage, family, and friendships. The practice of Management by Objective (MBO) measured the quality of one's work and the quantity of one's work output against the boss's previously stated objectives. For some, the familial atmosphere that had long epitomized office settings started to change, and despite such allowances as casual Fridays, in many companies work environments reflected a formal mindset: all business, all the time.

## Energy

The October 1973 Yom Kippur War was the mother of all socioeconomic game changers; the twenty-one day war and its immediate aftermath recast how the world related to the exploration, development, and use of energy.

As Israeli Defense Forces responded to the air and ground assault by Egypt and Syria, and as fighting escalated, the price of energy, particularly crude oil, skyrocketed. Always cheap and plentiful, crude oil was the lubricant of world economies; the pre-war average price of gasoline was thirty-nine cents per gallon. Then, in a flash, a significant portion of the world's oil was embargoed by an obscure energy cartel led by kings and sheiks and sultans of oil-producing (anti-Israeli) Arab nations, such as Saudi Arabia and Kuwait. This union became known as the Organization of Petroleum Producing Countries, or OPEC for short. By July 1974, OPEC's grip on global supply helped drive up the price at American service station pumps to an average of fifty-five cents per gallon, a 43 percent increase in just eight months.

In its initial response to the instant disruption of foreign crude oil supplies, the U.S. could do little more than the immediate, draconian steps it took to reduce energy consumption; Federal law lowered the national speed limit to fifty-five miles an hour; thermostats in offices, schools, and homes dropped to sixty degrees; and during the winter of 1973-74 Daylight Savings Time was scrapped, and children across the U.S. walked to school in pre-dawn darkness.

Detroit automakers, caught completely unawares as their market shares eroded, affected a frantic response to Japanese nameplates like Toyota, Nissan (previously Datsun), and Honda that manufactured the small, fuel-efficient cars Americans were growing to appreciate and buy in great numbers.

This energy crisis continued through the remainder of the administrations of Presidents Richard M. Nixon and Gerald R. Ford. Upon entering office in 1977, President Jimmy Carter became the country's most visible champion of renewable energy; his administration mandated new programs, encouraged resource conservation, and fostered energy research and development in technologies that collected solar energy by way of photovoltaic cells. To provide a visible symbol of his commitment to what was then known as alternative energy, President Carter installed solar panels atop the White House.

In the 1980 presidential election Ronald Reagan scored a landslide victory over President Carter, and U.S. based renewable energy projects lost their champion in the White House. Government funding for research and development ground to a halt, and the country's position as the world leader in renewable energy was threatened. In 1986, as part of a planned White House renovation process, President Reagan ordered the removal of President Carter's solar panels.

As the 1980s progressed, the "malaise" President Carter used to describe the nation's circa-1979 sour mood had become largely forgotten, replaced by newfound optimism and a sudden appetite for larger, more powerful cars. To satisfy the spike in demand, consumption of foreign oil—much of it from OPEC member nations—increased dramatically.

Iraqi President Saddam Hussein's invasion of the tiny oil-producing nation of Kuwait on August 2, 1990 and the Gulf War that followed in early 1991 reminded the industrialized world just how dependent it was on foreign oil, and how much of it is produced by nations that do not like them very much. The outcome of the Gulf War's thirty-four-day air and ground campaign codified a U.S. policy that assured America's continued dependence on, if not increased appetite for, foreign oil. Scant attention was paid when Saddam set fire to the oil fields of Southern Iraq and Kuwait. American consumers gleefully flocked to automotive showrooms to buy sport utility vehicles (SUVs) and trucks. During the 1990s, SUV and trucks sales led the entire automotive industry.

Big, powerful cars were in, fuel economy was out.

But in the 1990s, while the nation migrated back to big cars and trucks, some of the world's leading academics gathered alarming evidence that suggested a more ominous threat. There was growing concern among the world's esteemed scientists and climatologists that continued and growing use of fossil fuel had forced upon the planet a greenhouse effect; studies pointed to the steady rise in the earth's temperature that coincided with dramatic melting of the polar ice caps. In 1997, fearing that doing nothing would cause catastrophic, irreversible damage to the earth and its ecosystems, several of the world's nations met in Kyoto, Japan to begin the process of mitigating—if not entirely stopping—global warming and the rampant rise in $CO^2$ production with the most stringent standards for conservation and environmental quality ever set forth.

As adopted by several nations on December 11, 1997, The Kyoto Protocol decreed dramatic reductions of greenhouse gas emissions through widespread conservation and the development of renewable energy sources. The then Republican Party majorities in the United States Congress strongly supported increased oil, gas, and coal production and exploration as well as increased use of nuclear power. Summarily, Congress rejected Kyoto.

Under Kyoto, the European nations, along with several in South America and the Pacific Rim, moved forward with their own aggressive renewable energy and conservation measures, while the U.S. saw its hegemony in alterative energy research and development completely evaporate.

After Brazil signed onto Kyoto, it embarked on wide scale research and refining efforts to produce ethanol. As a consequence of this choice, Brazilians endured higher taxes and cost overruns. Now, however, ethanol is the primary automotive fuel in that country and Brazilians now drive newer, smaller, more fuel-efficient cars.

Ethanol is the darling of U.S. corn-producing states and their elected officials. That is why ethanol production remains a contentious presidential election year issue. And critics point out that a great deal of energy and acreage is required to produce ethanol, making its marketing as a "green fuel" highly suspect.

In 1998, the OPEC cartel suffered karmic payback; wobbles in its crude output resulted in a huge global oversupply. This caused an extended and precipitous drop in the price per barrel. According to Inflationdata.com, the average inflation-adjusted price of a barrel of American (domestic) crude oil dropped to $15.77. As a result, the price of unleaded gasoline sold at American service stations plunged to inflation-adjusted historic lows. Here in the Northern Virginia suburbs of Washington, D.C., a gallon of unleaded gasoline sold for the unbelievably low price of seventy-five cents a gallon. Happy motorists, some driving large SUVs such as the Hummer H2, filled up their extended-range fuel tanks without knowledge or concern of the looming energy crisis that would soon follow.

By the end of the 1970s, the U.S. led the world in renewable energy innovation. But by 2008, the U.S. had completely lost its renewable energy leadership to other nations. Germany dominated solar power development. Spain focused on harnessing energy from wind turbines. And France led nuclear and tidal energy development. *New York Times* columnist Thomas Friedman offered a blunt euphemism to describe America's energy technology atrophy. He wrote in his July 4, 2009 column, "Well, China has gotten on board—big-time. Now I am worried that China will, dare I say, 'clean our clock' in E.T." Friedman stressed that the People's Republic of China was poised to eclipse the U.S. as a larger and more powerful world force in the development of renewable energy technology. As we struggle through a prolonged downturn and high unemployment, Friedman argues that China is grabbing up scores of renewable energy technology development projects and millions of employment opportunities that otherwise would go to companies in the U.S.

The outrage of the September 11, 2001 terrorist attacks on New York and Washington, D.C., and the two front wars in Afghanistan and Iraq that immediately followed returned energy to the headlines, while the oil-demand pendulum swung back and forth. During the early years of the George W. Bush presidency, and as Vice-President Dick Cheney held secret talks with chief executives of oil and energy companies, neither the White House nor the U.S. Congress pursued renewable energy research, development, or production.

But in 2007, with new majority representation in the U.S. Congress and gas prices climbing, mainstream media covered more stories and aired more interviews with experts focused on the nation's newfound interest in conservation and renewable energy.

By the spring of 2008, at the very fueling spot in Northern Virginia where gas had sold for seventy-five cents a gallon in 2000, the price rocketed to more than $4.50 a gallon. The American economy, so long dependent on foreign oil, faced a doomsday scenario: change how energy is created and used or, quite possibly, perish.

## Green Jobs, Red-Hot Controversy

For a period of about thirty years, from the mid-1970s to the mid-2000s, renewable energy jobs in the U.S. remained a rarity, with no measurable green job growth potential on the horizon. But by 2006 and 2007, the prospect of new green jobs appeared likely to become reality.

In July 2008, at the Democratic National Convention held in Denver, Colorado, speaker after speaker promoted economic renewal through wide scale renewable energy development and conservation programs to build a new green economy and create millions of green jobs. One month later at the Republican National Convention held in St. Paul, Minnesota, Republican Party Chairman Michael Steele uttered his now famous "drill baby, drill" call for increased oil, gas, and coal production, including exploration from places such as the pristine Arctic National Wildlife Refuge (ANWR).

The ensuing presidential election, which many voters in 2007 believed would be a referendum on President George W. Bush and the wars waged in Afghanistan and Iraq, had by mid-2008 turned into a referendum on stabilizing a downward-spiraling economy through the development of green energy and green jobs.

The election of November 4, 2008 was pivotal. No single event better exemplified the world's green paradigm shift than Barack Obama's election on that date as the 44th President of the United States.

Almost immediately upon taking office on January 20, 2009, the new president rolled out an economic agenda that was both breathtaking in size and thoroughly green in scope. Congress passed and President Obama signed into law the massive American Recovery and Reinvestment Act of 2009 (ARRA), which included as a key priority reengineering the American economy by fostering renewable energy from wind, solar, biomass, tidal, and geothermal sources, and promoting energy conservation.

On June 24, 2009, the U.S. Department of Labor announced that approximately one-half billion dollars of ARRA funds would be directed to programs offering workforce education and training for so-called green-collar jobs.

The issue of green jobs has not been sheltered from controversy; on September 5, 2009, President Obama's green jobs czar Van Jones announced that he had resigned his White House post. According to a September 8, 2009 story posted to the NPR.org Web site, "Jones recently came under scrutiny after it was revealed that he signed a 2004 petition questioning whether the U.S. government allowed the September 11 attacks to occur, and after remarks in which he used a derogatory word to describe Republicans."

## Corporate Social Responsibility

In the September 13, 1970 *New York Times Magazine* piece entitled "The Social Responsibility of Business is to Increase its Profits," the late Economist Milton Friedman wrote:

> [The businessmen] believe that they are defending free enterprise when they declaim that business is not

concerned "merely" with profit but also with promoting desirable "social" ends; that business has a "social conscience" and takes seriously its responsibilities for providing employment, eliminating discrimination, avoiding pollution, and whatever else may be the catchwords of the contemporary crop of reformers. In fact they are—or would be if they or anyone else took them seriously—preaching pure and unadulterated socialism. Businessmen who talk this way are unwitting puppets of the intellectual forces that have been undermining the basis of a free society these past decades.

Surely, given the current green paradigm shift, this 1976 recipient of the Nobel Economics Prize is spinning in his grave. For Friedman, the mere idea of the triple bottom line would be economic heresy.

Tragic events, such as the fatal 1984 methyl isocyanate leak at DuPont's Bhopal, India plant and the massive 1989 Exxon Valdez crude oil spill into Alaska's Prince William Sound, became economic game changers as effective worldwide product boycotts took hold. Corporations that once poured raw sewage and toxic chemicals into rivers and streams, or that ran sweatshops in third world countries without much public outcry, are recognizing that an increasing number of consumers are intolerant of companies that hurt the environment, perform inhumane product tests on animals, and exploit underprivileged people.

Twenty years after the Exxon Valdez disaster, thousands of companies from industries as diverse as financial services, paper manufacturing, grocery and specialty-retail, and software development, are becoming stalwart practitioners of corporate social responsibility.

On his Web site Mallenbaker.com, corporate social responsibility expert Mallen Baker offers this tidy definition:

> CSR is how companies manage their business processes
> to produce an overall positive impact on society.

This brings us to one not obviously green company out front in its practice of CSR, global accounting and consulting powerhouse Deloitte.

Juliana Deans is the director of community involvement for Deloitte Service's San Francisco offices; she oversees the CSR volunteer projects of Deloitte's accountants and other management executives in regional offices throughout the Northern Pacific states, Alaska, and Hawaii. She also counsels Deloitte's senior management on neighborhood philanthropy opportunities.

Deans indicates that Deloitte's CSR efforts are especially effective because they are based on skill-based volunteering, which leverages associates' financial accounting skills to help revitalize inner city neighborhoods, reduce homelessness, and empower underprivileged people with critical workplace skills to render them productive and engaged members of society.

AT&T has teamed up with social media provider YourCause.com to launch a fully interactive nationwide Web 2.0 social community called AT&T Cares. The program "empowers each employee to further harness the power of technology and the Internet to champion causes that they are passionate about." AT&T Cares allows each employee secure access to the YourCause.com platform and a variety of Web-based tools that are provided within each personalized page. The AT&T Cares program makes employee volunteering convenient, fun, and truly meaningful.

In Washington, D.C., firms like RTC Relationship Marketing, industry trade groups, and other businesses dependent on the Federal establishment provide employees a few days of paid leave each year for volunteering; some employees tutor at-risk children in D.C.'s public schools, while others remove trash like truck tires and car batteries from the murky banks of D.C.'s heavily polluted Anacostia River.

Seattle-based Hacker Group boasts an active Philanthropy Committee, which auctions employees' arts and crafts for cash donations to local charities, assembles the Easter gift baskets provided to children living at local shelters for victims of domestic violence, and matches the cash contribution each employee makes to a cause of his or her choosing.

Deloitte, AT&T, and other companies that are not obviously green make a huge impact on their communities through CSR; as a result they provide their staff a source of personal pride and channels for community engagement that they may not have otherwise had.

It is within these not-so-obviously green companies where I believe executives can most easily join the ranks of The Green Suits. While the jobs they hold may not be obviously green like chief sustainability officer, a VP of finance or a senior director of purchasing would still be quite capable of personal sustainability achievements at work that make a big, profound, and positive impact on the environment.

Suppose you are, say, a VP of client service who has direct reports. By allowing your staff to take part in full-time or part-time telecommuting, providing them access to virtual office technology (such as video-conferencing and secure file-sharing), and full or partial mass transit subsidies so that they commute by car less, you are helping to significantly reduce your company's carbon footprint. Further, by designing and managing volunteer programs for your staff that leverage their skills and talents to aid and empower the less fortunate, you help establish and expand your company's corporate social responsibility bona fides. Simple steps such as these can turn your not-so-obviously green job green.

With an eye on establishing long range career goals, codify your green leadership by factoring sustainability and CSR objectives and successes into annual MBO reviews. That is part of Abhi Vyas' executive evaluation; his accomplishments on the job are measured in part by the effectiveness of his search engine optimization and social media efforts promoting MetroMedia's greenness and by the number of handbags and accessories Vy and Elle creates by using recycled Metromedia outdoor ads. MBOs are a great way to monitor and fast track your success as The Green Suit in your company.

# Chapter 2:

## Gather "Fabric" of Your Green Business Executive Career—Education and Training

The promise of green jobs has created a lot of excitement. Executives who are eager to join the fast-growing renewable energy and green tech spaces are flooding companies with résumés.

The problem is, as job seekers, we don't know what we don't know. Hiring managers who have open assignments tend to seek only the most qualified talent. As Tracy Crawford from Technical Green points out, "candidates lacking required [green] training and education won't get hired."

In March 2009, the National Environmental Education Foundation Business and Environment Program published *The Engaged Organization: Corporate Employee Environmental Education Survey and Case Study Findings* report. Among the landmark study's findings were these:

- 65 percent of respondents (hiring managers) value job candidates' environmental and sustainability knowledge;

- while 78 percent believe that the value of job candidates' environmental and sustainability knowledge will increase in importance as a hiring factor within five years.

And *Clean Tech Job Trends 2009*, an October 2009 study authored by Ron Pernick, Clint Wilder, Dexter Gauntlett, and Trevor Winnie, suggests an important factor relating to the need for green business executive training and education: "driving the trend is an unprecedented alignment of leading stakeholders—universities, trade groups, companies, and students."

Education and training are The Green Suit's cohesive stitches. That is why you must have a solid education and training plan in place before embarking on your green business executive job hunt.

There are three parts in the education and training pyramid that The Green Suit must continually assess: information, knowledge, and accreditation. As illustrated, a C-Suite will demand that its executives possess knowledge on a wide range of green, sustainable, and corporate socially responsible matters, while various institutions and social media channels will drive information, knowledge, and accredited degree programs to those executives.

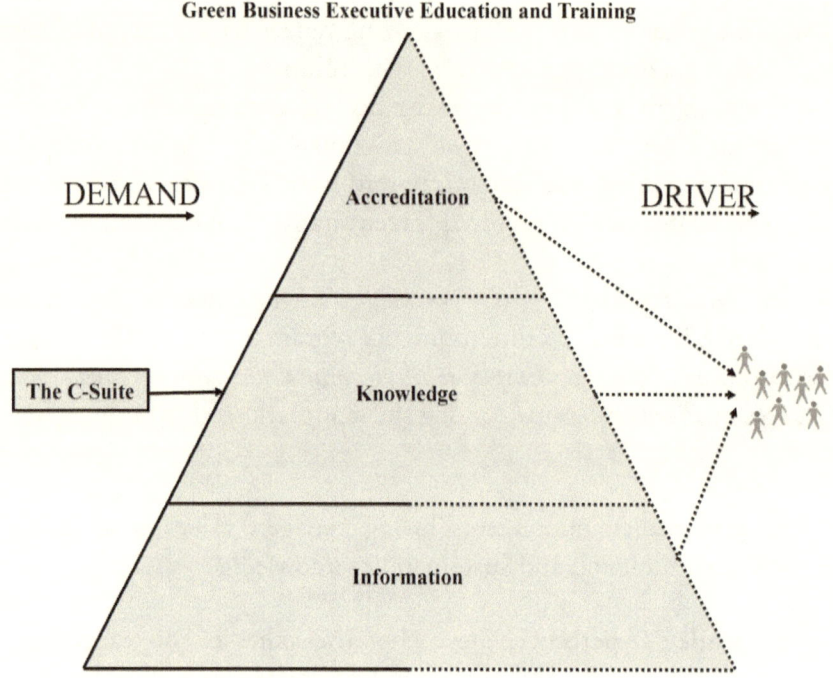

## Gather and Analyze Information

Information will be the foundation of your green business education and training. It is also the easiest to come by; informational resources you need or will come to rely upon may be available for free (or a nominal fee) by way of the Internet through green-related social networks. There is a lot of information to be found, covering subject matter as diverse as tidal energy technology and climate change mitigation. Start each business day by scanning the Web sites and communities that most reliably offer the information you need to understand the current issues and challenges affecting the green business space. Then explore areas of specialty, such as geothermal energy technology, forestry stewardship, or other areas that interest you most.

Not sure which information resources to use? The good news is that a few key words entered into most search engines will point you to scores of resources offering a lot of information (much of which will be current).

Expand your access to information by becoming a member of a trade association or business networking group that caters to your areas of interest. There are several that advocate for key industries within green business. These include, but are not limited to:

- American Wind Energy Association;
- Business Council for Sustainable Energy;
- Efficient Windows Collaborative;
- Geothermal Energy Association;
- Organic Trade Association;
- Solar Electric Power Association;
- Solar Energy Industries Association;
- Sustainable Buildings Industry Council;
- Sustainable Forestry Initiative; and
- U.S. Green Buildings Council.

What is more, there are new social communities forming every day—as stand-alone Web sites or in online social communities such as LinkedIn and Facebook – that may provide valuable information through article reprints and topical blog posts. *Check 'em out!*

And of course, the mainstream media remain channels for news and often useful information. Online outlets of *The Wall Street Journal, Barrons, Financial Times of London, CNBC, The New York Times* and its Green Inc. blog, and other major operations are more frequently covering stories on the green business front. Most of these outlets offer access to their content for free or a nominal fee.

Not all information rises to the level of knowledge and so it is important to maintain a respectful skepticism about whatever you read, hear, and see. What is reported or offered as information may be nothing more than hyperbole. This is why I am skeptical about referring executives to sites that have not proven to be useful. Even if something is seemingly credible and it is from an otherwise reliable source, it may not be useful. However, you will discover that a lot of the information out there is valid and will most definitely enhance your green business expertise.

## Acquire Knowledge and Experience

Committing yourself to perpetual education and training is critical. Your understanding of green jobs, green companies, and the green economy will change and change rapidly. And what passes as adequate knowledge now may be inadequate in a matter of years, or even months. Executives who adapt accordingly will thrive, and they will receive the most benefit from this education and training.

Joe Boudreau is a director of business development at Babson Executive Education, a phenomenal executive training resource that *Business Week* ranks as the sixth best provider of custom executive education programs in the U.S. It is located fourteen miles west of Boston, Massachusetts on the campus of Babson College (itself a world-class institution for entrepreneurial studies). Through his work with senior executive clients, Boudreau is keenly aware of the importance knowledge plays in the corporate world, and of the importance of embracing the new green paradigm.

Boudreau says that the knowledge requirement often starts in the C-Suite where the CEO, CFO, and others mindful of government oversight and regulation demand that their senior executives remain up-to-date on green business-related issues. These C-level executives must ensure that their corporation remains among the world's top green companies and in full compliance with new environmental regulation. He points to the experiences many companies faced in the aftermath of the 2001 Enron collapse and the resulting passage of the Sarbanes-

Oxley Act; practically overnight, C-level management at public companies had to comply with added layers of government-financial oversight and tough new regulations to avoid the dire consequences of non-compliance.

Further, Boudreau notes, "We are seeing the same kind of urgent demand from the C-Suite, this time to assure their boards that senior management obtain the knowledge they need to comply with potential initiatives like Cap and Trade."

Babson Executive Education has developed a world-class reputation for providing executives actionable knowledge to fully overcome the many challenges faced by corporate management. While many of the current executive education offerings can be modified to include the implications of the green paradigm shift, Boudreau expects the amount, diversity, and sophistication of green business-related course offerings and content to grow quickly.

Given the current economic climate, it is apparent that some executives will have to self-fund their acquisition of new skills. However, in the years to come, I believe corporate America will increase funding for executive education programs. Recognizing that knowledge is an important business requirement, savvy CEOs, CFOs, COOs, and CMOs will gladly invest in their executives to secure their future success.

Knowledge also is available through online webinars. The great advantage of webinars is that an executive may log on and learn anywhere in the world and at any time. While live webinar events do not offer literal face-to-face engagement, some do allow one-on-one dialogue (between lecturer and online training participant). Webinars can be cost-effective and very convenient; some are free of charge, others are available for a nominal fee, but the ones that provide the deepest and most useful knowledge taught by the world's most highly respected green business leaders may cost an attendee several hundred dollars or more. Since attendees don't have to travel great distances by air or by road, or require hotel guest accommodations, webinars help save thousands of dollars in corporate travel and entertainment expenses. And using webinars affords the executive substantial carbon footprint reductions.

If your webinar participation is related to a career change, your out-of-pocket expense may be tax deductible. Check first with your accountant or tax advisor before claiming any income tax deductions for career-related training.

So far, there is no consensus for what is actionable knowledge and experience. According to CA's Steve Boston, among sustainability officers there "is no commonality of experience." Boston says that sustainability management executives possess a wide variety of specialized skills: IT; finance and risk management; economics; marketing; and the physical sciences, to name a few. And the kinds of sustainability knowledge these executives seek is influenced by their own "discipline-weighted problem solving." Surely as corporate sustainability becomes more widely established, you can fast track your career while setting the path for future green business executives to follow.

For the time being, not every executive will be willing to make a three, four, or five-figure investment in non-accredited certificate programs to gain useful green business knowledge. In order to acquire experience, some downsized executives who have limited financial resources are taking the unusual step of accepting non-paying internships at obviously green companies and organizations. Internships have grown in popularity because they offer executives very specific hands-on knowledge about what many consider work requirements for green managers.

The rules for internships? So far, there don't appear to be many. And that may provide enough flexibility to an executive eager to quickly fill green gaps in an otherwise stellar résumé. Contact internal recruiters at the companies that interest you to determine if they have green business executive internship programs.

## Gain Accreditation

From the entry-level executive eager to embark on a green business career, to the more seasoned management executive looking to leverage his or her skills and talents as part of the green business revolution, the importance of education and training cannot be overstated. This is *the* constant, the career-long investment essential for success.

During the 1970s—in the wake of Watergate and following the release of both the book and the movie *All the President's Men*—colleges and universities across the U.S. reported a bumper crop of undergrads enrolled in journalism degree programs. In the 1980s, tens of thousands of MBAs entered the corporate ranks. In the 1990s, and as a result of the Internet Age, men and women received bachelors, masters, and doctoral degrees in information systems in large numbers.

Now, as the Green Paradigm Shift takes hold, undergraduate and graduate degree programs in environmental science, environmental policy, renewable energy, sustainability, and corporate social responsibility are growing in popularity. American institutions of higher learning as diverse as the Arizona State University, Bates College, Georgia Tech, Harvard, and SUNY Binghamton are featured on Princeton Review's Green Honor Roll.

According to a news release on the school's Web site, "Arizona State's School of Sustainability, W.P. Carey School of Business, and the Hugh Downs School of Human Communication have collaborated to provide course content required for the new Bachelor of Arts degree in sustainable business. This new degree, which will be awarded beginning in 2012, will help graduates and future business leaders leverage some of the best practices in sustainability."

Aside from Princeton Review's top picks, there are hundreds of other excellent institutions, such as the University of Maryland at College Park, George Washington University, and Babson College, that are strongly committed to educating tomorrow's green leaders.

Babson Executive Education's senior director of business development Joe Boudreau believes that MBA degree programs concentrated on sustainable enterprise should be the goal of The Green Suit. He says that accreditation that combines an excellent MBA program with the best knowledge from the renewable energy and sustainability fields will help The Green Suit fulfill his or her greatest potential. Sustainable MBA degree programs are offered by a handful of institutions, including: Presidio School of Management, Dominican University of California, Green Mountain College, The University of Colorado at Denver, Antioch University of New England, and The University of Michigan (which, in particular, combines its MBA degree with a masters of science in environmental studies).

Education, however, is not just for newly minted green executives;

it also provides great benefits for experienced executives in other fields eager to enter the green business space.

After two years of classes and a full-time work schedule, Kas Neteler received her MBA in sustainable enterprise from The Green MBA® Program at Dominican University of California. A senior art director for many years, Neteler decided that staying in the publishing industry, which is so heavily dependent on paper, would be a career ender. Further, she wanted to "explore more executive levels in an organization." The Green MBA provided her excellent leadership training from Dominican's "holistic program," which focused on triple bottom line thinking.

Like a lot of us, Neteler reached a point where her career and her life goals disconnected. Growing up in a modest home where dinner table discussions centered on business at the family's car dealership—but never about over consumption—she found in the Green MBA program that going green provided her opportunities for integrating the "authentic lifestyle" she experienced as a child (her parents practiced sustainability and social responsibility) with a rewarding executive business career.

Tuition reimbursement for accredited degree courses may also be available through your company, and most large companies also provide training. Even if your company does not offer green training, sometimes by networking with a top trainer you may identify the most appropriate green business-related training tracks to pursue.

Over the years I have looked at thousands of résumés, and now I receive many from Millennial-aged graduates. I am struck by how many of the Milliennials have earned degrees in green, sustainable, and socially responsible fields of study. The Millennial Generation is our most green and socially conscious generation, so it is no surprise that so many Millennial-aged graduates embark on green careers. Green degree accreditation will provide them with a solid foundation for their future green education and training.

But what about the rest of us who have been in the work world a few years longer and do not possess the requisite green accreditation? How will those of us willing to go back to school to earn green degrees?

It won't be easy, especially for those of us who work full-time jobs, but millions of dollars in ARRA funding soon to be directed towards advance-level training and new accredited degree programs may make attainment easier and more affordable.

While a large chunk of that ARRA funding will be directed towards community colleges for so-called green-collar job training and accreditation (e.g., trade specialties such as weatherization), many new educational opportunities at four year schools are being developed expressly for green business executive careerists. In March 2009, Congressman Zack Space presented to the House of Representatives an appropriation bill to further expand green business-related degree accreditation.

Pursuing green degree certification mid-career is a noble goal. Green business accreditation is still relatively new. And with so many schools opting to develop green course offerings, it may not be easy to determine which accredited program best meets your needs. Take the opportunity to ask questions of admissions officers, and, if possible, speak to some recent grads to gain insight and gauge their satisfaction.

As The Green Suit, it will be critically important for you to periodically take measure of yourself. In the short term, no one will expect you to be expertly informed, but hiring managers will value executives who are willing to further their education and training for the betterment of the corporation. So, do commit a portion of your work schedule to reading, listening, absorbing new information, and attending seminars and webinars. And if you have the means and the desire, pursue accredited degree programs that meet your requirements.

The flood of green jobs in sectors such as renewable energy and conservation has yet to materialize. But soon we should see a noticeable increase in green business executive job postings. That is why it is important to recognize now that you don't know what you don't know. If you are serious about a pursuing a green business career, then use your time wisely to start becoming well-informed and well-trained in green business practices. Starting now will provide you clear advantages over other job candidates possessing little or no education, training, or experience.

As you gain more education and training, remember to adjust your personal management-by-objectives (MBOs) upward and pointed toward greater career challenges. And keep in mind that while your green skills are important, so too are your non-green career-related skills. Make certain that they remain current and well-communicated in your résumé. (More on that subject follows in Chapter 3.)

## Politics vs. Green Business Executive Career Education and Training

As a result of the Obama administration's and Congress' emphases on green business, the concept of green jobs has become—and will continue to be—politically charged. Some of us advocating for a green economy and green jobs—green business executive jobs—have become reluctant politicians. Since President Obama's inauguration, my SturdyRoots.com blog has been flypaper for trolls whose commentary characterizes the green economy and green jobs as "foolish," "selfish," "crazy," "socialist," and worse. Being a green business pioneer requires thick skin.

Among the political pundits and 501c3 political action committees are those defending the status quo: some say that green energy development is a boondoggle, that there is enough crude oil in the ground to last centuries, and that the U.S. should not be leveraging tax dollars to fund renewable energy and sustainability technologies that have not yet gone to market.

One group, ironically called $CO^2$ Is Green, uses its Web site to claim that broadly accepted scientific (global warming) data are *myths* propagated by industries with financial interests. According to the group's Web site, "Humans inhale and exhale $CO^2$ with every breath. How could anyone expect you to believe it is a human health hazard?" and "The inconvenient truth: the world is now cooling, not warming."

Some pro-green activists and advocacy groups have labeled Republican Senator James Inhofe and others in Congress climate change deniers and "flat-earthers." In a January 4, 2005 speech delivered on the floor of the U.S. Senate, Inhofe described global warming as "the greatest hoax perpetrated on the American people."

The U.S. Chamber of Commerce, the world's largest business federation, has voiced strong and sometimes fierce opposition to Congressional climate change legislation. In the fall of 2009, in an effort to quell rebellion within its ranks, the Chamber moderated the tone of its disapproval. Chamber chairman Tom Donohue, as quoted on the Chamber's Web site, claimed that, "the American business community *would* welcome legislation. [We have] not ruled out all cap-and-trade systems or a carbon tax." Yet, two formidable energy companies, Exelon Corporation and PG&E, joined a growing list of members quitting the Chamber because (as reported on September 29, 2009 by *The Wall Street Journal, The Washington Post*, and other news outlets) the Chamber remains in opposition to climate change legislation.

Then there is the research paper published early in 2009 titled *Green Jobs Myths*, co-authored by Andrew P. Morriss of The University of Illinois, William T. Bogart of York College of Pennsylvania, Andrew Dorchak of Case Western Reserve University, and Roger E. Meiners of the University of Texas-Arlington. The study's authors address "myths" behind many green jobs claims, refute the notion that green jobs will increase employment, and echo the challenge described earlier in this book that "no standard definition of a green job exists."

And last, but certainly not least, there was the mother of e-mail bombshells that some call "climate gate."

On November 20, 2009, London's *Guardian* newspaper was one of the first to report that "hundreds of private e-mails and documents allegedly exchanged between some of the world's leading climate scientists during the past thirteen years [had] been stolen by hackers and leaked online." Climate change skeptics and deniers claimed that information hacked from computer servers owned by the University of East Anglia, a leading climate change research institution, provided "smoking gun" evidence that some of the climatologists had colluded in manipulating data "to support the widely held view that climate change is real."

Meanwhile, in a *New York Times* story posted on November 21, 2009, NASA climatologist Gavin A. Schmidt, whose e-mail exchanges were among many leaked, responded to the controversy claiming "science doesn't work because we're all nice" and "Newton may have been an ass, but the theory of gravity still works." And in his December 1, 2009 post, *New York Times' Freakonomics* blogger, author, and economist Steven D. Levitt concluded that the "e-mails aren't that damaging" and "academics work behind the scenes constantly trying to undermine each other. I've seen economists do far worse things than pulling tricks with figures. When economists get mixed up in public policy, things get messier. So it is not at all surprising [to me] that climate scientists would behave that same way."

While the actions taken by these scientists were foolish, I remain convinced there is sufficient untarnished scientific data available to conclude that global warming is indeed real. Still, like a beat reporter gathering facts, you too should remain respectfully skeptical of anything you hear or read. When appropriate, ask tough questions of people who make green claims. Don't take any information at face value. Thoughtful probing and persistence will force us all to be better informed, help us better defend our beliefs, and make us better green business leaders. Doing so will help us verify what we know.

Whatever your political orientation—left, right, or center—remember that what matters most is that green is good for business. It is a given: billions of dollars in government financial resources are going toward, and will continue to be appropriated for, green energy research and development, technological advancements, and business expansion. What is more, CEOs across the business landscape have accepted that the green economy is real; on September 28, 2009, John W. Rowe, Exelon's chief executive officer, joined a growing list of companies quitting the U.S. Chamber of Commerce by proclaiming: "the carbon-based free lunch is over."

Those of us who use our time to passionately seek knowledge and information—to improve our green business career successes—will succeed. Those who continue to naysay or who are late to the gate will not. Let us all learn and become well informed so that together we lead this green business revolution.

# Chapter 3:
## Taking Measure—Seeking Out, Landing, and Creating Your Green Business Executive Job

Once you have established and begun pursuing a solid education and training plan, you may begin seeking out and landing green executive employment, pursuing a not obviously green job that could be turned green, creating a green job for yourself in your current company or another non-green establishment, or adding greenness to the job you already have.

But before you start updating your résumé, there are a few steps you need to follow first to take measure of yourself and your career objectives.

## Establish Your Value Proposition

Before you begin the job hunt or make any modifications to your current résumé, it is important to first take the time to establish your value proposition so that you articulate well what it is you bring to a company to help turn it green (or greener).

Your value proposition will become critically important as you pursue your green business career, because so much of the green business revolution is about attitude. Certainly, a hiring manager will want assurance that your head will be focused on achieving critical program objectives or improving return on investment, and he or she will also look to determine that in your heart you are committed to creating a better, greener world.

Being able to articulate your value proposition will help you connect your core competencies to your career objectives. It will empower you as you interview for and land new executive assignments, and it will enable you to visualize future long-term success. Senior management who fully understand and appreciate your value proposition will turn to you for insight and advice on achieving corporate green goals. And that advantage will lead you to a better, more satisfying career track offering more frequent promotion opportunities, higher salary and greater benefits, and recognition of your accomplishments by senior management.

So how do you establish your value proposition?

Begin by making a checklist of all that motivates you to pursue a green business executive career. Examples could be:

- a desire to help a business improve its sustainability;

- wanting to provide well for myself and my family by doing well for the planet; or,

- leveraging knowledge of green and sustainable practices to help empower others to do the same.

This is your reason for being; if you remain mindful of your value proposition you will continually meet and exceed your career-related objectives. Also, you will further your reputation as The Green Suit—the reliable and passionate executive who can deliver on the job.

## Write or Revise Your Résumé

We know that hiring managers are more positively predisposed to the best green trained and educated talent. A busy hiring manager may have an inches-thick a stack of résumés to review, and he or she may give any of those documents a spare twenty-five-second glance. There is no denying that good résumés elicit more immediate and positive response while not-so-good résumés often get tossed in the circular file. This document can open doors to a new job; understanding that it includes valuable real estate will help you make it a more effective job-landing asset. If through strategic use of the résumé real estate you communicate well your business career story and your greenness, chances are the hiring manager will respond favorably.

What information should you include on your résumé? Since your core objective is to get noticed by a green executive hiring manager, you need to use the real estate well to communicate your express green business executive career objectives, key green accomplishments, green or sustainability-related training and education, the greenness of your work assignments, and metrics—lots of metrics.

A truly outstanding résumé will quantify your professional career accomplishments and help the hiring manager answer questions such as these:

- How much new business was the executive personally responsible for generating in the previous year or year-to-date?

- How large is the executive's current operating budget? How much has it grown in the past three years?

- How large is the executive's head count? How many of those people are direct reports? How much has the executive's head count increased over the past three years?

- How much of the operating budget has the executive recouped? How much of the savings are attributable to the executive's energy and resource conservation efforts?

How should you organize the information on your résumé? You have three main decisions here—whether to use a chronological or functional format, what to put on the first page, and whether to use key words.

First, should you present your information chronologically or according to function? Susan Ireland speaks to this issue. She is one of the U.S.'s foremost authorities on résumé writing and the author of *The Complete Idiot's Guide to the Perfect Résumé* and *Ready-Made Résumés* software. She is a frequent blogger, a well-respected speaker, and her Web site SusanIreland.com is an important destination for anyone needing sound résumé-writing advice.

Ireland says that, "since the 1980s, résumés have gone through an evolution." Back then, use of the chronological résumé as presentation-of-choice began to wane as MBA-earning business executives opted for the unorthodox functional résumé format. Where an old school chronological résumé may have dryly answered the where and when of the executive's work history, the new format provided the executive the means to project uniqueness by detailing core competencies, special or unusual skills, and career goals and motivations.

Ireland recalls that by the 1990s "it seemed as if the functional résumé was working, especially if the executive had work history problems." That is because the functional résumé could enable a business executive to shine while downplaying the absence of any key skills, a pattern of short (two years or less) job assignments at different companies, or the presence of not-easily-explained timeline cavities. Yet many hiring managers and executive recruiters grew suspicious of candidates relying on this type of presentation.

Now, Ireland says, most business executives favor a combination résumé format that provides chronological details but also showcases the executive's skills, accreditations, and accomplishments.

Secondly, what should you put on the first page of your résumé? The old adage of real estate agents—that the three most important considerations are location, location, location—applies equally well to an executive careerist's résumé. When crafting your résumé, be mindful of the real estate agent's mantra. The details you need to communicate most—and most effectively—should appear prominently on the first page.

Throughout my executive recruiting career I have often relied on unscientific review and recall experiments to gauge the effectiveness of newly arrived résumés. Using a test subject who happened to be a hiring manager, I would place before my test subject (face-down) a never before seen résumé. On my mark, the test subject would flip the résumé over and begin reading. At the twenty-five-second-mark, which happens to be the approximate amount of time I find hiring managers take to scan a résumé, I would ask the test subject to stop reading, return the document face-down, and recall as many candidate details as possible.

What occurs quite often with test subjects is this: I watch the eyes begin at the top of the résumé then quickly scan down to the bottom of the first page. Then the eyes dart back to the top of the document.

If the information is of interest to the test subject, invariably he or she will peek through the other pages to seek out secondary details such as prior work history and education. If not, the test subject may impatiently remain on the first page, scanning from top to bottom, side to side, until the exercise concludes.

Invariably, what the test subject recalls best and most accurately are the data provided at the top half of the first page (the prime real estate), followed by the data at the bottom half. If during the twenty-five-second exercise the test subject's interest is aroused, then he or she may well recall less-prominent details.

## Résumé Reading and Recall Exercise

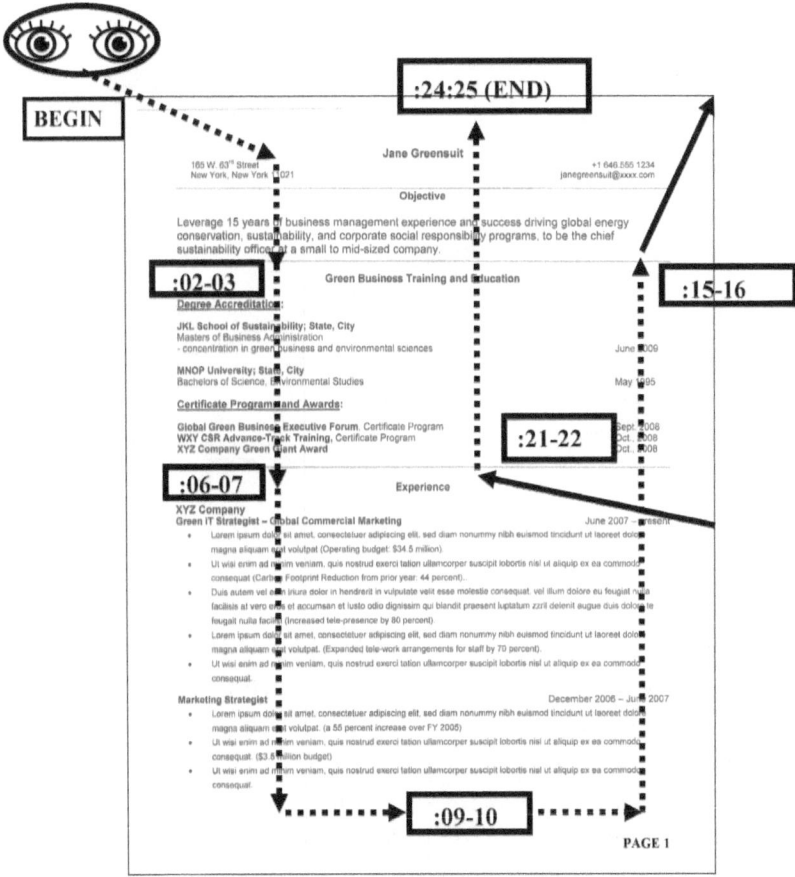

Invariably, a seriously interested test subject will continue on to the subsequent pages in the résumé:

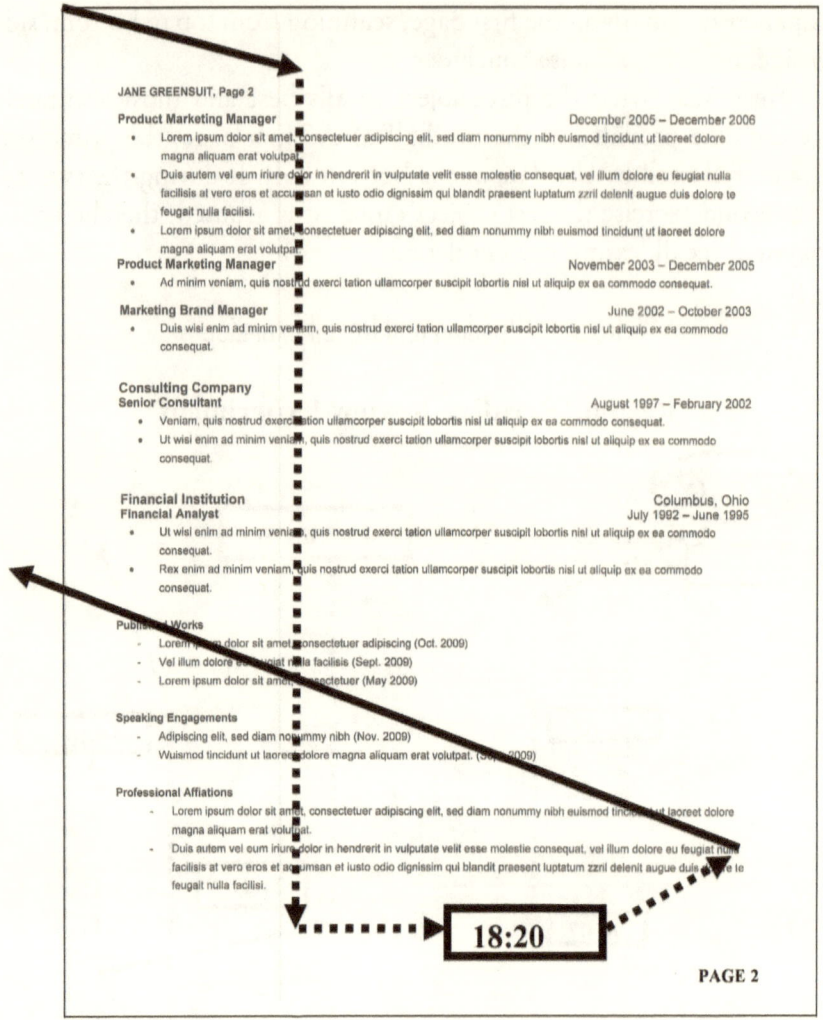

I mention this review and recall experiment to show that in order for your résumé to get noticed, your first page should contain your career objectives, key accomplishments, applicable training and education, and recent career history.

Thirdly, there is the issue of key words on your résumé. Quite often, corporate internal recruiting departments are besieged with candidate responses to even a single job posting. To triage the tonnage, internal recruiters may rely on software that scans key words in résumés to find possible candidate matches. This has led some candidates to add stand-alone key word sections to their resumes. For fear of tackiness alone, I counsel candidates against doing that. It is my experience that key word sections in a résumé raise red flags; when spotting them corporate recruiters may conclude that the candidate is more of a generalist than a green business specialist. Indeed, that old expression applies: "Jack of all trades, master of none."

Knowing that companies will do what they need to do to balance candidate review with time and cost considerations, a candidate should prepare by reviewing the posted job specs and the company Web site; if you notice, for instance, that the company you are about to solicit specializes in carbon sequestration and that is one of your many areas of specialization, then by all means include "carbon sequestration" in your résumé.

And it should go without saying, but I'll mention it, anyway: *do not* add key words to your résumé that are not reflective of your experience or areas of knowledge or accreditation. Including them may get your résumé flagged for initial follow-up, but later in the vetting process it will likely shoot down your candidacy.

Please indulge me while I state the obvious: do not send out your résumé unless and until it has been carefully spell checked. I often find that the résumés of more-seasoned executives contain a greater number of typographical errors than the ones from less-seasoned executives who typically have the most current job hunting experience.

If you believe your résumé is out of tune and you need a fresh "voice" to maximize your appeal, seek out a reputable résumé writing service or purchase a high-quality software utility. And if you are an aspiring American expatriate seeking an executive career opportunity in the European Union or the Pacific Rim, you should know that résumé (or curriculum vitae) writing practices are often quite different from the American ones. If you plan to work outside the U.S., I recommend contacting an international résumé writing service. One such resource, CVWrite.co.uk, helps American expatriates transform their résumés into highly effective curriculum vitae, especially ones tailored for green business executive careers that are across the pond or around the Pacific Rim.

To further paraphrase the old joke in Chapter 1, gather six executive recruiters to determine the best way to prepare a résumé and they'll come back with seven answers. So leverage the experience and insight that executive recruiters and résumé-writing experts like Susan Ireland may provide. But develop a style and presentation that suits you, The Green Suit, best.

## Peruse the Job Boards

Over the past two years, several commercial job boards have been launched that offer assignment postings expressly for green professionals. These include: CareerEco.com; GreenCareerCentral.com; GreenJobs.BrightGreenTalent.com; TechnicalGreen.net; Jobs.GreenBiz.com; and GreenProfs.com. Several trade associations, including the Solar Electric Power Association and the American Wind Energy Association, have launched their own job boards. And the mega job boards—CareerBuilder, Monster, and HotJobs!—post green executive opportunities as well. There are many channels already available to the green executive job seeker, and many more to come online soon. And that is good news indeed.

Further, there are some novel new Web sites that aim to make the xx more enjoyable, and perhaps more effective, for both the candidate and the hiring manager. VisualCV employs a Web 3.0 approach, empowering each candidate to post a graphic-rich CV or résumé to their site that might also include video attachments prepared by the job seeker. VisualCVs are downloadable as PDF files (for easy viewing). Candidates certainly could use this tricked-out vehicle to effectively communicate their greenness.

There is a downside to having so many good job boards launched; as of this writing, there still are only a limited number of green business executive job postings to populate these sites. One may find that there are very few assignments exclusive to one job board or another, and that scores of executives apply to the same jobs.

## Contact Companies, Strategically

Unsolicited calls to a company's internal recruiter may seem like an effective way to find a green business executive assignment. However, most internal recruiters are overworked and time-strapped. Often, phone calls and e-mail messages from people they do not know may get a delayed response, or remain unanswered.

Neysa Bennett, a successful executive recruiter and principal of Bennett Baker Group, is nationally regarded for her expertise in corporate hiring best practices for the direct and interactive marketing industries. She agrees that internal recruiters and human resource personnel are often besieged, adding, "If you decide to contact a company directly, you need to do so strategically. Suppose you discover [there is a great green job] at a company that immediately interests you, or you have heard that a company may be a great place for an aspiring green business executive to work. Without a doubt, the best way to get into that company is to work your business and personal network. You may know people who know people in the company, and they in turn may lead you to a hiring manager." Absent a connection to a company networking contact, Bennett suggests reaching out to the most senior hiring managers, as they may know of appropriate opportunities.

## Build Your Network

Networking is critical to your job search; it requires a substantial investment of time, but it is well worth the effort. Whether done at business luncheons, during after-hour wine and beer mixers, or online in green business social communities, networking will provide you with the best opportunities to engage with other green business executives. Meeting them, you may learn about green executive jobs that interest you—and best of all—that have not yet been publicized. And you will definitely gather a lot of information about new technologies and emerging companies that may expand your career options.

There are dozens of ways to build a network, but this chart illustrates some of the channels you may consider to build yours:

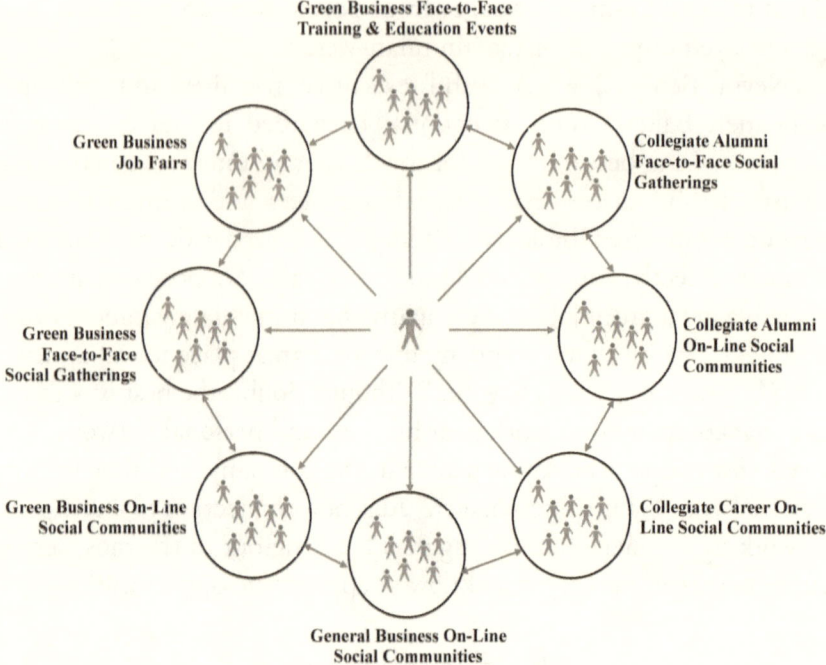

Sometimes I hear from executives that because of social anxiety, they shy away from attending networking events. That is a terrible mistake. If shyness affects you, strive for ways to empower yourself and overcome this obstacle. Ask someone you trust to help you strategize ways to break the ice and initiate conversations with people you don't know. Chances are, many if not most of the people you meet at green business networking events are also new to the space. (And some of them are shy, too.)

## Consider Blogging

For someone like me who writes a lot, blogging is a fun means of self-promotion. Starting a blog is easy; well-visited blogging communities such as Blogger.com and Wordpress.com allow you to launch an aesthetically pleasing, feature-rich blog in minutes, for free.

Veteran marketing communications expert Lauretta Harris of Write

Communications believes that if you write well and have something interesting or useful to contribute, then blogging may greatly expand your network and job-hunting by showcasing your green bona fides.

Harris says that "the point is to remain on the [green business] radar in a memorable and positive way." But she warns, "When it comes to blogging or writing an e-newsletter, remember that most green business professionals are reading the same Web sites and getting the same information [as you]." Harris says to avoid reprinting news from another blog or online news and information source, which she calls "flogging the blog." Unless you are able to add your own memorable points or suggestions, "you'll just be training your prospects to avoid you."

Although not inherently green business focused, I do make a point of reading veteran Chief Marketing Officer Randall Beard's blog, RandallBeard.wordpress.com, regularly. It showcases Randall's talents as a world-recognized CMO and presents well his unique point of view on business, brand identification, and marketing best practices.

## Engage with Executive Recruiters

There are not a lot of executive recruiters focused on green business at the moment, but that is sure to change once the economy improves and scores of new green executive jobs come to the fore.

Executive recruiters are indeed excellent resources for The Green Suit. Some have entered recruiting after careers on the other side of the table—as management in renewable energy, green/clean tech, sustainability, green marketing, and CSR—and possess deep knowledge of the green business space that will serve your interests well. They have solid relationships with a wide range of green businesses and will be keenly aware of the requirements of open assignments, some of which may be exclusive executive placement offerings. What is more, since they possess intimate knowledge of their clients' operations, they are well suited to guide executive candidates through the prolonged interview process through successful negotiation and job placement.

Placement fees are paid by the hiring manager, not the candidate. If someone claiming to be an executive recruiter indicates that you, the candidate, must pay the placement fee then please do not hesitate to *hang up the phone.*

Some executive recruiters have developed résumé-writing services on the side, the fees for which are paid by the candidate (and that is entirely appropriate). As with any information and training you require, do ask probative questions. Skepticism on your part is healthy.

## Prepare for Job Interviews

In some respects, interviews for The Green Suit are no different than for any other candidate: they establish core competencies and subject matter mastery and determine if his or her personality and temperament complement those of other team members or provide a good but underperforming team a much-needed boost of energy.

But in other respects, The Green Suit's interview experience may be quite different: The Green Suit must use the interview to establish credibility; personal familiarity with sustainability, conservation, and CSR best practices; an understanding of the regulatory landscape; and other challenges. And, because The Green Suit is an ambassador for the new green economy, he or she must also communicate a fire-in-the-belly passion for the environment and the public good.

Technology has become more sophisticated, prices have dropped, and new tools have come to market that allow hiring managers, recruiters, and candidates separated by thousands of miles the experience of virtual face-to-face interviewing. While some technical glitches are bound to happen, hiring managers using Web-based video interviewing technology have told us that they like this added interview process dimension.

Service providers such as InterviewStudio.com offer solutions that provide hiring managers ease of use and flexibility. They may also allow the candidate to participate from any video-enabled personal computer. For hiring managers, these relatively inexpensive services allow them to take a peek before committing substantial long distance travel and hotel expenses for on-site face-to-face interviews.

Tandberg and Lifesize Communications provide technological solutions with high-definition sound and video quality that may be appropriate for remote interviewing senior-level candidates. While hiring managers employing high quality tele-presence services may find the experience to be satisfying and convenient, certain technological considerations may necessitate that a candidate conduct his or her end of the interview from a remotely located professional video facility, rather than from a personal computer.

## Establish an Interview Strategy

Preparing for any executive job interview requires the candidate to conduct thorough research. Often an executive recruiter or coach will suggest resources beyond the company Web site to study. These may include news articles, financial data, C-level profiles, and other information.

One area where an executive recruiter or coach may prove valuable is in how they prepare you for the personalities you will encounter. You'll learn from these professionals the unique styles of their hiring manager clients: some hiring managers like to do most of the talking, they may use a significant portion of your interview session to share details of the assignment while asking few questions about you and your qualifications. Other hiring managers may seem as thorough as an attorney in the courtroom. They may rattle off a quick succession of probative questions and you do your best to answer each of them, succinctly. A good recruiter or coach will share what they know about the hiring manager to prepare you well for the interview experience so that you come across crisp, confident, and well prepared.

As The Green Suit, the value of your training and information gathering will be of critical importance to the hiring manager; he or she needs to be assured that your skill can be leveraged immediately.

If all goes well and you have demonstrated that you are indeed the right candidate for that green executive job, then congratulations! An offer will be forthcoming.

But before you even get to the offer stage—perhaps as early as your first engagement with a recruiter or a potential hiring manager—be prepared to discuss your expectations of base salary, upside from bonuses and sales commissions, and other remuneration. In other words, what you require to accept an offer. But be reasonable: currently, this is a buyer's market which means that there are more job seekers than there are jobs. If your compensation requirements are deemed to be too rigid or outrageous, then you may lose that sweet green business executive assignment to someone else.

## Create Your Own Green Business Executive Job

If a new green assignment is far from reach, then creating your own green job—or adding greenness to the job you already have—may be a solid plan for you, The Green Suit, to accelerate your green business career.

There are many green-minded executives who like the small or medium-sized companies where they work and admire and respect management; they share the company's general vision, goals, and strategies, but feel that their companies are missing opportunities to leverage their creativity and talent to foster a green culture and sustainable business practices. Instead of leaving for greener pastures, these enterprising executives have convinced their hiring managers that they are the right people to manage these verdant goals. And in doing so, they have created their own green business executive jobs.

And what a win-win that is. Ambitious green-minded executives are advancing their careers by acquiring measurable sustainability experience for themselves and profound improvements for their companies.

Due to continued uncertainty about the economy, you may be inclined to stay where you are. Or you may enjoy your company and its culture. That considered, you may feel that there is more that you could be doing to further your company's sustainability focus and achievements, or your own green bona fides. If you have determined that the best career strategy is to stay where you are, consider building a case to present to your hiring manager to create your own green job. Your presentation to management should answer questions such as these:

- What are the company's green pain points (energy efficiency, sustainability, CSR) that you could overcome?

- What are the green goals you believe your company should be seeking to mitigate these pain points?

- Why are you the executive to make these improvements happen?

- What are the financial or budgetary considerations?

- How do you propose to measure your success (cost savings, carbon footprint reductions, community improvements, et al)?

- What internal or external resources will you need to meet and exceed these goals?

- When should you assume these responsibilities?

- Where will you be based (a traditional office setting or virtual office)?

- How do you propose to be compensated? And how might upside compensation (from bonuses) be tied to goal attainment?

Almost all of the largest companies (certainly those in the Fortune 500) and many of the medium sized ones already have sustainability programs in place. But that is less the case in small companies, which make up about three quarters of all U.S. businesses. Pragmatically speaking, if you work for a very small company (up to fifty employees), these new green responsibilities may need to augment your current job requirements. If you are in a company of between fifty to one hundred employees, then it may be possible to create your own job focused exclusively on green and sustainable goal attainment. Either way, you assume the role of the de facto sustainability executive in your company.

Good experience is necessary for a successful business executive career. And if you don't possess sustainability-related degree accreditation or have yet to complete important green business executive certificate programs, then you will need to rely on your on-the-job experience—

shaping and securing your company's goals and successes—to build the foundation for a successful and personally satisfying green business executive career.

# Chapter 4:

## Pressing The Green Suit's Corporate Culture

As The Green Suit in your company, you may assume considerable responsibility for thought leadership on renewable energy, greentech or cleantech, sustainability, and corporate social responsibility. And to a certain degree you may become your company's ambassador to the new green economy: the evangelist for best practices, the debunker of myths, and the strong bottom-line-focused executive.

For many companies, sustainability and return on investment seem to operate at cross-purposes. But as The Green Suit, you will take on this winnable challenge to show your senior management and the entire enterprise that a company can do well by meeting and beating financial forecasts, but also do right as passionate environmental stewards and socially responsible neighbors.

## Things You Can Do to Establish Corporate Greenness

- Be the champion of tele-presence. Recognizing the vast impact on the bottom line, most large global corporations now have a tele-presence. Important meetings that used to involve flying executives long distances and across multiple time zones are now staged with ease. Executives in settings as large as town hall-sized events or as small as home offices may, with a couple of mouse clicks, get linked together to create a single high-quality experience. Most importantly, tele-presences save corporations millions in annual travel-related costs and may create a new standard for how some executive candidate interviews are staged. Companies such as 8x8 have included excellent video capabilities as part of their IP telephone systems, while high-end providers Tandberg and Lifesize Communications offer technological capabilities that lend intimacy to multi-point virtual meetings.

- Subsidize sensible commuting solutions. Get corporate buy-in to cover all or part of your team members' mass transit commuting expenses. Subsidy programs in the Federal government sector have proven successful by encouraging van-pooling and train commuting which has removed tens of thousands of cars from highways and secondary roads and helped contain airborne emissions. Push for the creation of a green fleet that pollutes less and provides the best fuel efficiency, and includes hybrid and partial-zero emissions (PZEV) vehicles. Or, move your suburban company back to the city: Massachusetts-based renewable energy company First Wind recognized that its suburban Newton location was a turn-off to its mass transit favoring talent. So, the seventy-employee company moved its offices within Boston city limits to a location a short walking distance from South Station. Employees who may have needed a car for the reverse commute to the old location in Newton are now using public transportation to get to work. Similarly, interactive marketing communications agency Hacker Group energized its mostly city-dwelling staff when it relocated from suburban Redmond, Washington—the hometown of Microsoft—to downtown Seattle.

- Commit to doing more than safe, toe-in-the-water green practices. Develop programs that go beyond office paper, bottle, and can recycling to create measurable sustainability and energy efficiency improvements. Hacker Group has done something quite impressive: the firm composts almost all of its cafeteria waste. The agency's new Seattle offices employ motion sensor activated electrical, plumbing, and heating ventilation and cooling (HVAC) systems that save considerable energy and water resources.

- Chart your company's ongoing carbon footprint reductions. To that end, employ the kinds of readily available tools that allow carbon footprint reduction to take place. Employ easy-to-use computer power management software from Verdiem and other manufacturers, and connect to the power grid with the aid of smart electric metering technology. Place your company's carbon footprint reduction map in prominent places and gathering points to remind staff of their accomplishments and how resulting cost savings translate to higher corporate bonuses, ROI improvements, and more staff hiring and retention.

- Take the lead in promoting corporate social responsibility by following the examples of companies such as Deloitte and Target, which promote skill-based volunteering. It used to be that corporate involvement in social responsibility went only as far as employee participation in annual United Way campaigns. But as we know, CSR is becoming a very hands-on affair that draws in executives with various skills and talents. Identify a dozen or so projects in your community—from trash removal to carpentry; from feeding, clothing, and teaching the less fortunate to installing high-speed Internet bandwidth at inner-city schools—that can generate immediate goodwill and make your company's neighborhood more livable. A very worthy organization, Habitat for Humanity (habitat.org), operates in many localities and provides executives high impact and newsworthy ways to extend corporate social responsibility.

- Draw in nature's beauty and create hospitable ecosystems that attract hummingbirds and other species by adding work campus gardens. Management may look critically at the cost of such projects—a program to plant eighty thousand trees around one corporate campus was declared dead on arrival when management got wind of the program's high six-figure cost estimate—so develop plans that have limited impact on the bottom line. Considerable savings are possible by purchasing small seedlings that grow quickly and are appropriate for your climate zone. For instance, here in the metro Washington D.C. area, many businesses choose tree species that need little to no care and feeding to thrive, such river birch and weeping willow. Both species are ideal for sensitive wetland areas. And for hot, sunny spots near asphalt-covered surfaces, drought-resistant fast-growing shrubs such as burning bush or succulents such as sedum are commonly selected for their seasonal beauty and year-round durability.

- Empower staff by extending sustainability education and training opportunities to the entire company. Extend education and training to show how meeting and exceeding compliance goals will translate to measurable ROI improvements while encouraging more bottom up idea generation and top down empowerment strategies and best practices. During the next few years, a multitude of education and training resources will come to market, and it is likely that some of the specific programs offered may be customized to meet your company's express requirements.

- From the start, strive to make every job in your company a green job. We know that the Millennial generation is producing a bumper crop of sustainability-minded executive talent. So push your company's hiring managers and human resource heads to include individual and group sustainability and corporate social responsibility goals in every job description. Then, urge them to include attainment of these goals in periodic MBO assessments.

- Remind the C-Suite of the value of continued sustainability and corporate social responsibility efforts, and challenge them to set aggressive attainment goals. How your company becomes and continues to be bright green sets the stage for great public relations opportunities and helps increase consumer demand for products and services. As noted in Chapter 1, roughly 80 percent of consumers have a positive opinion of green products and services and of companies that, to some degree, practice sustainability and corporate social responsibility.

- And last, establish a permanent and enduring culture of transparency in your company. CA's Steve Boston knows how difficult it is for any publicly traded company to embrace transparency, especially when success in the market may hinge on maintaining some cloak-and-dagger secrecy. Boston says that "[transparency] takes some getting used to" and that CA stepped up and, he believes, is as transparent as it can be. As a result, the powerful message that CA embraces transparency, "building technologies to help [our company] run better," gets communicated well to customers, equity holders, and the community.

## Create Your Own Advisory Board

Establishing yourself as The Green Suit is critical to establishing and expanding your company's greenness. But as easy as some of the previous steps may seem, there are potentially some large obstacles that may make achievement difficult (and in some organizations, close to impossible).

That's why I suggest that you create your own advisory board, a group of senior green business executives skilled in various aspects of business operations, training, and of course sustainability and corporate social responsibility, to help you overcome any looming roadblocks to success.

Advisory boards are key components of many emerging businesses, especially ones that have experience cavities, meaning that key personnel may not possess all the critical skills and experience necessary to achieve success. Personally, I think having a team of trusted experts guiding you and watching your back may be one of the best ways to achieve and exceed the green goals you have established for yourself and your company.

A well-selected advisory panel will help you and your company pivot into the green business space faster and with greater success. Further, your panel will help you bridge the all-too-common gap between will and skill. You may be your company's most ardent supporter of sustainability, but without the skill learned from—and guidance provided by—an advisory panel, you may fall short of your objectives to become The Green Suit.

## Get on the Fast Track to Understanding Regulation

We enter the green business world encumbered by considerable regulatory oversight. C-Level executive in companies whose businesses affect the world's resources are anxiously awaiting news of the kind and severity of regulation that Washington has in store. Many companies will require their top management to gain mission critical knowledge quickly so that they are in compliance of these new regulations.

As The Green Suit in your company, you may be called upon by senior management to receive training necessary to mitigate the effects of increased environmental oversight. I mentioned earlier that one resource, Babson Executive Education, is developing customized programs to make sure management teams are well educated and that they have the knowledge to manage their companies through the uncertain terrain of new environmental regulation. Being well informed and well educated in sustainable practices and environmental stewardship is the best way to press The Green Suit's corporate culture.

Whether at Babson's program, or at countless others offered by accredited colleges and universities, become aware of the ways you—The Green Suit—may receive the knowledge and training necessary to assure that your company complies fully with governmental regulatory oversight and remains at the forefront of sustainable and CSR best practices.

## From the Bottom Up: Gain Staff Input on Sustainability

Recognizing that some immediately actionable measures come from within the ranks, many corporations encourage staff suggestions for improving corporate sustainability. Here are some notable results:

- At Yahoo!, green team members' "Chuck the Cup Day" promotion discouraged continued use of disposable paper cups. Members handed out fifteen hundred green ceramic mugs to employees at Yahoo! offices in Sunnyvale and Burbank, California.

- eBay's green team constitutes roughly 10 percent of the total workforce. A suggestion provided by one of its Salt Lake City team members is already in practice: preferred parking at the Salt Lake City facility is now provided to employees driving fuel-efficient vehicles.

- In San Mateo, California-based eMeter's green team has surveyed employee transportation habits to measure their carbon footprints, and has identified barriers to employee use of more mass transit and carpooling.

CA carefully considers sustainability proposals it receives from its talent across the globe. Only those proposals that score best in 1) reducing CA's carbon footprint, 2) minimizing operational costs, 3) enhancing CA's positive reputation in the global community, and 4) improving ROI are implemented.

As The Green Suit in your company, you will be the change agent responsible for the creation and implementation of many solid, measurable, and truly impressive programs. But be mindful that within your company there may be a considerable number of skeptics who don't see the value in your initiatives. Surely, articulating a strategy that balances the triple bottom line will not be an easy task. But over time, and as you showcase your company's successes, you will win over many skeptics.

Not only will you have a considerable role in reducing your company's carbon footprint and extending its corporate social responsibility deeper into the community, you will also greatly expand your own career prospects.

# Chapter 5:

## If the Suit Fits ... WEAR IT!

Being The Green Suit, you do well by doing right. But your sphere of influence need not end at the company gate.

Ample opportunities abound for you to engage audiences outside of your company, to showcase your company's green success stories, and to gain recognition as a noted expert—a public advocate for sustainability and corporate social responsibility.

If the suit fits, WEAR IT!

As you develop your green business executive knowledge, skill, and experience, work to increase your visibility and industry's recognition of you as The Green Suit. Here are some things you can do now to maximize your efforts:

### Perfect Your Three-Floor Elevator Pitch

Bedazzled by our iPhones, Blackberries, Bluetooth headsets, and other mobile commuting devices, we executives are more time constrained and distracted than ever.

Unlike executive counterparts in other parts of the globe, American executives tend to define themselves by their work. In Europe, it may be considered rude to ask someone you do not know what they do for a living. But in the U.S. it is likely that that question will pop up in conversation between two executives meeting for the first time.

According to the Web site GottaMentor.com, a good elevator pitch communicates *why* you are someone worth engaging in conversation. Its effectiveness depends on presentation, but also on how many of the "Seven Elements of a Good Story" you use, and how well you use them. They are:

1. Industry relevance;
2. Communication skill;
3. Leadership experience;
4. Problem-solving skill;
5. Expertise;
6. Pedigree; and
7. Impact.

Employing as many of the seven elements as possible, an effective elevator pitch might sound something like this:

> Good morning, Ms. Forest. My name is Gwen Verdant and I believe that I would be an engaging speaker at this year's regional business conference.
>
> I launched Acme Insurance Corporation's nationally recognized sustainability program. During the past four years I built it from scratch into a department with a two million dollar budget—and direct accountability to the CEO—to generate over fifty million dollars in energy and resource recycling savings. Plus, I led one of the region's largest corporate volunteer programs—a very successful urban renewal project that planted one hundred shade trees in blighted neighborhoods.
>
> As you can see, I am eager to share these successes with the business community, and was wondering if we could meet to discuss how I might lead a green business focused session at the conference?

For some, starting a first-time conversation such as this may prove to be a difficult challenge. Preparation and practice to make the pitch sound natural and unrehearsed are key, thus I counsel boiling down that elevator pitch to three floors (about thirty to forty-five seconds). Doing so will help break the ice in an otherwise awkward encounter, expand your professional network, increase sales leads (if you are a green business sales executive), and of course engage you in conversation with a future hiring manager who is immediately impressed by the succinct way you presented your green bona fides.

Engaging people you don't know can be difficult, especially if you find yourself self-conscious or shy in group situations. But having a well-honed three-floor elevator pitch will help create opportunities that may lead you to great achievements in your green business executive career.

As The Green Suit, you are an ambassador for green business and green business executive employment. Keep that three-floor minimum in mind when an executive you meet for the first time asks what you do.

## Speak at Professional Meetings and Conferences

And as you develop a reputation of success and achievement—and perhaps employ a three-floor elevator pitch such as the one illustrated in the previous section—you may be asked to participate in speaking engagements outside your company at industry conferences and other business gatherings. I suspect that green business focused conference promoters—especially ones that cater to local or regional business audiences—may call on you to leverage your express talents and areas of expertise by addressing audiences and participating in interesting panel discussions.

Mark Twain once said, "But [I] was never happy, never could make a good impromptu speech without several hours to prepare it." Good public speaking requires lots of acquired skill and practice. Toastmasters International is a phenomenal resource that helps empower executives with the skill and confidence needed to give great speeches and presentations. For the less practiced speaker, Toastmasters provides the instruction and guidance needed to overcome the jitters and other awkward or off-putting verbal and nonverbal habits. The organization has established local chapters in many U.S. cities.

## Write Columns and Opinion Editorials for Business Publications

Throughout my career, I have found that writing columns and opinion pieces provide great opportunities to promote my areas of expertise. In the past five years, several of my op-eds have appeared in the Fredericksburg, Virginia *Free Lance-Star* newspaper and my monthly "Ask the Headhunter" column appeared in the Direct Marketing Association of Washington's *Marketing AdVents* publication.

And now that most news and information is available online, it is easier and faster than ever to get your pieces published.

Especially in an area as new as green business—where every day, we get to write the narrative—crafting columns and op-eds allows you to be The Green Suit before large audiences of fellow professionals. One excellent resource, TheExaminer.com, provides excellent opportunities for professionals to write about their areas of expertise and the issues and challenges that affect them at work.

There are many timely green business issues that would make excellent topics for a printed or online op-ed. However, if you struggle coming up with topics that interest you, then consider these:

- Ten steps to running a successful virtual office.

- Promoting employee use of mass transit.

- Sign me up! Encouraging your most stubborn employees to embrace corporate volunteerism.

- I've replaced all the old light bulbs. Now what? Five great opportunities to turn your company green.

- Developing a corporate social conscience—ten things your company can do to be a force of good in the community.

What your three-floor elevator pitch can do in one-on-one encounters, editorial writing may do on a grander scale. And don't hesitate to reach out to general interest publications, which likely will be interested in what you have to express and provide access to a broad and very interested readership to boot. Not everyone is lucky enough to get a letter or an opinion piece published in *The New York Times*. But you will likely find that smaller, regional publications (both print and electronic media) consider your writing interesting and worthy of publication.

## Mentor the Green Suits of the Future

Certainly, speaking engagements may extend to the college campus. As the Millennials prepare to enter the workforce, they will actively seek advice from successful business executives. Since this generational cohort is so highly predisposed to environmental stewardship and eager for mentorship, many of these soon-to-be-graduates may be The Green Suits of the future. How might a green executive engage such audiences? How might mentorship work? Would you be successful in enticing ambitious undergrads to accept internships at your company?

Stuart Katz is president and executive producer of Elm City Communications, a leading corporate marketing communications company based in New Jersey. For many years, he has been an ardent proponent of undergraduate internship programs; corporate communications college students participating in Elm City internships gain valuable hands-on learning that serves them well once they enter the executive and professional ranks. Katz has found the internship experience satisfying for both him and his students. In fact, one of his former interns is an Elm City Communications executive.

Katz is also an adjunct professor of corporate communications at Seton Hall University; as an expert producer of webinars and other distance learning tools, he has provided his undergraduate charges an immediate understanding of and appreciation for these verdant technologies which they can use at future jobs to reduce travel costs and their company's carbon footprint.

## Promote Green Business Executive Job Fairs

As much of the national conversation has centered on green jobs, most of the job fairs taking place across the country, such as the California

Green Jobs Summit, have a generic green jobs focus. And that needs to change.

As The Green Suit, you are uniquely qualified to promote job fairs that benefit aspiring green business executives. Encourage companies you work for or do business with to sponsor job fairs that may attract green business executive talent. Because of the economic downturn, job fairs are very well attended, providing hiring managers great opportunities to engage scores of future green hires who—as a result of attending an event—discover the skills and experiences they need and the education and training required to land a rewarding green business executive job assignment.

## Walk the Walk

As a business executive and as a consumer, The Green Suit needs to remind the rest of the world of the power and importance of being green by walking the walk and talking the talk. It is easy to show others how easy it is to live and work in a more sustainable fashion. Here are a few practices that you as The Green Suit may consider to demonstrate your greenness:

- Ditch the bottled water in favor of filtered water. Many of us already use some form of home water filtration, such as Brita filtered water pitchers or PUR faucet attachments, which make ordinary tap water taste as refreshing as spring water. A new product called Clear2Go is a water bottle with a built-in filter. It is perfect for the office or for whenever you are on to go.

- Cut down on dry cleaning. Dry cleaners use harmful solvents such as perchloroethylene or perc. To make matters worse, the clear poly bags cleaners use to wrap cleaned and pressed clothes effectively trap concentrated perc vapors which can get breathed in (once the bag is opened). Perc, in wide use since the 1940s, is a known carcinogen. It is my experience that most business wear needs only a quick steam and press to be wearable. But if you must spot-clean your garments, do so using non-toxic products. Dry clean only as a last resort.

- Favor mass transit. Not all Green Suits have access to reliable mass transit, but if possible, you should ride the rails or board the bus for your daily commute. Mass transit provides a welcome break from driving, ample opportunities to complete some office work, or, my personal favorite, time for power naps. Take every opportunity to persuade the executives you encounter to make mass transit subsidies available at their companies. If at all possible, favor trains over planes when you travel long distances to business meetings and industry gatherings. Instead of hailing a taxi cab, walk to your next meeting. If the circumstances are favorable, consider riding your bicycle to the office. And if you require use of a car, chose a make and model that gets great gas mileage and reduces carbon-based emissions, such as a hybrid partial-zero emissions vehicle (PZEV).

- Show others how easy it is to track your carbon reduction success. Carbon footprint reduction Web sites are as easy to use as they are numerous. Some of the most popular ones are offered by clearmetrics.com, carbonfootprint.com, and zerofootprint.net and offer the capability of tracking home versus business carbon footprint reduction. And since most of us access the Internet on mobile communications devices, it is easy to show executives in other companies what great strides you have taken at home and at work to reduce your impact on the environment.

- When making presentations to clients, prospects, or outside groups, select presentation materials made from recycled content and other sustainable materials. As The Green Suit, *how* you present yourself to the outside world may be as important as what you present. If you must provide leave-behind material, take care to make sure it is comprised of recycled or sustainable content. Grossman Marketing Group manufactures and sells a full line of business accessories such as computer cases made from recycled plastic and computer jump drives encased in bamboo—one of the most sustainable wood products. Recycled products tend to cost more than their conventional counterparts, but prices are falling enough that the difference between conventional and recycled or sustainable will soon be negligible.

- Make yourself a public spectacle. As The Green Suit, you may wish to speak at the open sessions of local, state, or federal government meetings to promote issues of particular importance to green business such as policies that bring green jobs closer to where people live. For instance, before a gathering of local, regional, or state elected officials you could promote the idea of bringing private enterprise, accredited institutions, and government together to bring well-paying executive employment—green business executive jobs—directly to your city or county.

Here is how I have made myself a public spectacle: on my community's local cable access news shows, in newspaper interviews, and on my blog, I have proposed that some of our esteemed green focused Virginia colleges and universities—College of William & Mary, Virginia Tech, University of Virginia, Hampton University, et al—open satellite campuses here to draw in innovative green tech companies and the green business executive talent required to operate them. Government aids the effort by providing incentives—some in the form of tax reduction or abatement—to open offices, factories, and other facilities in the community. I happen to like this idea, because it is fashioned after the three-legged table approach used to create model successes like Research Triangle, North Carolina. In my community it would help diversify an economic base that is heavily dependent on the defense industry. Such diversity helps communities mitigate unemployment when an industry suffers a major setback. Using the three-legged table approach to draw in green business helps raise awareness and interest in renewable energy jobs that in turn would entice green accredited executives to live and work in my community. One favorable aspect of this approach is that it provides relief to communities—such as those in the American "Rust Belt"—still reeling from decades of double-digit unemployment and so many industrial plant closings.

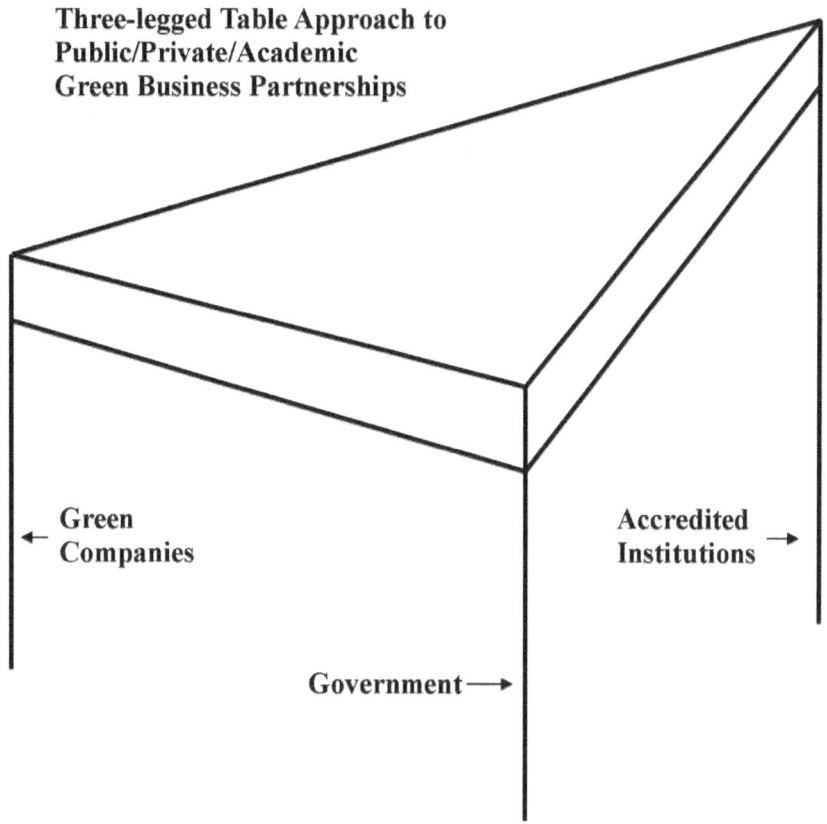

- Take the stairs. Help reduce energy consumption while demonstrating to others the benefits of taking the stairs over that elevator trip. And in the process, turn your three-floor elevator pitch into a three-floor staircase pitch. Plus, the stairs provide a great way to get in your daily cardio workout.

- Let that summer lawn turn brown. To paraphrase Monty Python's classic Dead Parrot comedy sketch: "[It's] not dead, [it's] resting!" Well-established lawns may lose the rich, green color of springtime, but during the hot summer months they go into a dormant (resting) state. Watering lawns during the hot months prevents them from setting deep roots, while rendering them more dependent on water from irrigation. Even if set properly, lawn irrigation systems can heavily deplete local watersheds and hasten government-imposed water restrictions during periods of summer drought. I suggest getting rid of some of that lawn and replacing it with low-maintenance shrubs and trees that, when mature, will provide your home with shade that will lower your home's electrical load. If you must, water your plantings in the early morning when air and ground temperatures are coolest.

- When shopping, bring your own bags. This is one of the most visible ways to show your greenness. For my weekly grocery run, I bring along two large, oblong canvas bags that have handles. That translates to as many as a dozen plastic shopping bags saved per shopping trip, over six hundred annually. At stores where I may need only an item or two (easily hand-carried) I tell the cashier I do not need the bag. The good news is that bringing your own bag has never been more convenient. Most U.S. grocers and retail chains sell inexpensive, reusable canvas shopping bags;

- Clean up after your pet (immediately). Thirty years after Mayor Ed Koch began shaming his fellow New Yorkers to clean up their pets' waste, I am surprised to see so many people turn a blind eye to scooping the poop. If, like me, you live by sensitive wetlands, you should know that uncollected pet waste adds nutrients to ponds, streams, lakes, and rivers, robbing them of the oxygen fish need to live. So, when walking my dog, I always have a bag ready—usually a used plastic shopping bag—to immediately clean up his messes. Hopefully, others who see you being the good citizen will follow your example.

- Run your washer on its cold settings. Until recently, I did not know that most laundry detergents sold today work well with cold water. Plus, cold water saves hundreds of kilowatt hours needed to run your water heater annually. If you don't own one, consider buying a high-efficiency front-loading washer—featuring the EnergyStar® logo—which requires considerably less water and energy to run than conventional washing machines. And to save more energy, air dry business shirts and blouses and iron them as needed.

- Know your stuff. You lend the green business revolution great value by being a well-informed ambassador. Borrow a page from the pundits on television and have your talking points ready to discuss with interested executives or perhaps climate change skeptics. Best, know where to point an executive interested in reading useful and informative web-based articles and insight from research studies.

- Never pass up an opportunity for a teachable moment. Remember when you were eight or nine, how much you enjoyed learning about ecology? Children are no different today. Extend their passions by telling them about the work you do as The Green Suit. Career Day is still a big draw at school, so consider sharing with young audiences the important work done by green business executives like you. And think how satisfying it will be when during dinner, some eager third or fourth grader says to mom and dad, "I know what a triple bottom line is … do you?"

- And, for the benefit of all, show your enthusiasm. Very exciting times are upon us; don't be shy about letting loose the fire-in-the-belly enthusiasm you have for our green business future. If you enjoy writing, blog about your personal experiences. If you enjoy speaking, find a receptive audience. Whatever you decide to do, hold your head high as you walk the walk and talk the talk.

If you are like me, you will find that wearing The Green Suit and being a public advocate of the green paradigm shift is the most satisfying part of the green business executive experience. The work we do is indeed very important, but it is our positive attitudes and living by example that will encourage others to join the green business revolution. And perhaps our lasting legacy will be to finally show the world that business executives can still be motivated by profit while being powerful instruments for sustainability and corporate social responsibility.

# Chapter 6:

## Not Cut Out for Corporate Life? Fashion Yourself the Green-Suited Entrepreneur

Not everyone is cut out for corporate life. Some thrive only when being their own boss. The executives with a passion for sustainability and corporate social responsibility who start successful businesses are The Green-Suited Entrepreneurs.

Entrepreneurs drive innovation, and some ride their creative energies and business talents to multi-millionaire status. But it takes a lot of hard work, smarts, and good luck. The U.S. Small Business Administration (SBA) estimates that one out of every three start-up companies fail by the two-year mark while approximately 56 percent of all start-ups do not survive beyond year four. And given the current economic downturn, those odds will need to be adjusted to reflect higher failure rates. Many will fail, some miserably—that's the risk any entrepreneur assumes. However, thousands will strike it rich and enjoy a level of success beyond their wildest dreams. If you are a corporate escapee (by choice or by pink slip), you recognize in yourself the capacity for self-discipline and commitment to run your own business, and you have an appropriate amount of seed capital at your disposal, then becoming a Green-Suited Entrepreneur may be the spot-on career choice for you.

Green business entrepreneurs will produce the technologies and processes that change the world. And while today the energy tycoon T. Boone Pickens continues to grab the headlines and post the sound bites, all across the U.S. there are dreamers busy inventing our green future.

Are there green inventors somewhere out there in their basements and garages, tinkering on tomorrow's green innovations? Most definitely!

But inventors won't be the only Green-Suited Entrepreneurs: there will be millions of marketers, designers, merchants, sustainable crop growers, consultants, supply-chain professionals, and other specialists.

The Green-Suited Entrepreneur may assume several important roles at once. To name a few: business developer, marketer, inventor, sales executive, manufacturer, financier, and consultant. And here are some Green-Suited Entrepreneurs making an impact:

## The Pioneering Green Manufacturer

John Aker is President and CEO of Aker Wade, a company that has already developed a worldwide reputation for excellence in the area of electric vehicle (EV) fast-charging.

Aker's company is already the world's largest supplier of industrial fast-chargers. But his dream—and the program he is working on with the greatest of interest and effort—is designing, manufacturing, and bringing to market the electronic vehicle fast-charge station (in other words, the gas station of the future). With the Chevy Volt and other EV makes and models coming to market soon, there will be a need for stations where a driver may fast-charge his or her car's batteries quickly for the three or four hundred miles down the road.

Aker has taken on a daunting challenge. EVs require substantial energy load to fast-charge their highly sophisticated rechargeable electric fuel cells. But his company is making great progress and we expect that the world may soon get to know the name Aker Wade.

## The Green Marketer

Ben Grossman is a passionate green marketer and environmentalist. A member of the Millennial Generation, he represents the environmentally committed cohort entering the work world en masse. Although he is young, Ben has already gained a well-earned reputation for integrity and transparency with clients at some of the nation's leading consumer brands. What is more, Ben speaks regularly at green business gatherings.

And in 2009, he won a green business award from *Boston Business Journal*. He walks the walk and talks the talk.

Ben's company was founded in 1910 by his great-grandfather Maxwell Grossman under its original brand name, Massachusetts Envelope. At first, the company manufactured easy-to-use sealable pouches that thousands of newly arrived immigrants to the U.S. relied on to safely send money home to family members in Europe and other parts of the globe. Over the years, the company grew substantially and gained an excellent reputation for printing and manufacturing office materials of the highest quality: envelopes, letterhead, brochures, and other business collateral.

About fifteen years ago, Massachusetts Envelope was renamed Grossman Marketing Group (GMG) and its focus expanded to include marketing communications agency support services. And now GMG has a formidable green marketing practice run by Ben Grossman. The company employs a lot of green technology: envelopes are now manufactured using 100-percent certified wind-powered presses and envelope windows are made from biodegradable corn polymer to provide clients with best in class sustainable marketing materials. And as mentioned earlier, GMG manufactures and sells a full line of business accessories (portfolios, computer cases, and computer jump-drives) that are constructed out of recycled and sustainable materials.

Brad Davis is a highly successful green entrepreneur and virtual chief marketing officer. Davis is the former chairman of the retail advertising and marketing association division of National Retail Federation and head of Global Customer Engagement Strategy for renewable energy leader SunPower Corporation.

He is also a nationally known speaker on green and sustainable retail marketing; with over twenty-five years of experience providing customer-centric structures to leading manufacturers, service companies, and non-profit organizations, Davis helps consumer brands achieve maximum success in the new green paradigm. He is passionate about green business and working from a virtual office.

As he sees it, "Many green-motivated companies do not have a chief marketing officer and rely entirely on their marketing agencies and creative resources to fulfill the CMO role." Davis believes that this is a huge mistake. In his role as virtual CMO, he consults with senior corporate management, establishing go-to-market strategies that they can present to their agencies for execution. Davis continues, "This is important on two fronts: it assures that company objectives remain customer-centric and that corporate green initiatives are better realized."

An enthusiastic ambassador for sustainable and corporate socially responsible business practices, this green entrepreneur is able to make a huge impact on his clients' marketing and customer acquisition efforts, while helping them drive significant return on investment.

Jacquelyn Ottman is the founder of J. Ottman Consulting. As she explains it, "I got into this business twenty years ago when no one had ever heard of green marketing." Now, New York City-based J. Ottman Consulting is recognized as a world leader in green marketing and eco-innovation consultation. Her clients include many of the greenest companies on the planet: IBM, Nike, 3M Company, HSBC, and Rodale. And she is a noted instructor of graduate-level green course offerings and participant in green business roundtables.

## The Green Consultant/Collaborator

Earlier in the book, Kas Neteler described her life-transforming experience earning a Green MBA® from Dominican University of California. Previously an art director in the publishing industry, Neteler now has corporate leadership skill and knowledge gained from a business degree program that above all else values the triple bottom line.

As a result of the MBA program, Neteler gained an appreciation for core group business models and collaboration, which she and several other green MBA grads have used to form a new kind of business consultancy. The Idea Hive leverages specialties in research, workshop facilitation, consulting, strategic development, thought-leadership, creative direction, and other disciplines to empower individuals, businesses, and communities to "discover sustainable pathways forward."

## The Green Designer

West Coasters Andrew Soernsen and Mark Morris started Turk+Taylor to design, manufacture, and market well-tailored and sustainable men's and women's fashion. Portland, Oregon designer Gretchen Jones founded Mothlove which features high fashion created using sustainable materials and earth-friendly manufacturing processes.

And London native Nicola Freegard founded Vy and Elle, the company that takes MetroMedia Technologies' expired vinyl outdoor advertising sheets and transforms them into stunning fashion and business accessories such as handbags and cases for personal computers and iPhones. A lifelong environmentalist, Freegard repurposes the vinyl substrate material that otherwise would take up hundreds of thousands of cubic feet in landfill areas.

## The Virtual Assistant

I hear from many executives who operate from virtual office settings, and some of them struggle to make the arrangement work; one of the most common challenges they face operating from a virtual office is hiring support personnel to handle the various administrative and operational requirements of their business enterprises. One major obstacle is legal: some condo boards and homeowner associations prohibit commercial enterprise. Another headache is that homeowner insurance policies are not written to cover workers compensation.

Recognizing that she could turn such problems into opportunity, Samantha Mayfield established Starleaf Business Services. This Tulsa, Oklahoma-based company that provides expert virtual assistant support for enterprises across the U.S. Mayfield says her company "supports busy executives and business owners by taking care of e-mail, voicemail, meeting calendar updates; sending thank-you notes, special event cards and reminders; producing Microsoft Excel spreadsheets, Word documents, and PowerPoint presentations; and other tasks."

She adds that her virtual assistance allows executives more time to cultivate and close new business and attend to other important matters. As an outsourced solution, Mayfield's company eliminates costs frequently associated with employees: health coverage, 401k plan matching, and unemployment insurance.

## The "Climate Superhero" Motivator

Dave Finnigan is an expert motivational speaker. A few years ago, he grew "very concerned that the planet could have as many as three hundred million climate refugees" and that he needed to do his part to prevent that from happening. So Finnigan seized an opportunity to merge his motivational speaking expertise with the sustainability and personal responsibility-focused program he designed to move elementary school-aged children to do their part to save the earth.

Now, as founder and CEO of Climate Change is Elementary, Finnigan brings a full day of fun, guilt-free climate change instruction to public school classrooms throughout the Northeast, the Washington, D.C. metropolitan area, and California. With appearance fees covered by school parent/teacher organizations, he presents an innovative program that uses "the intelligences—kinesthetic, temporal/spatial, musical, and interpersonal learning" to turn young, eager-to-learn kids into "climate superheroes;" to help each teacher model new, effective teaching methods; and move parents and children to action, "to green the planet, together."

Like any enthusiastic entrepreneur, Finnigan saw a need and seized an opportunity to create a timely, in-demand educational experience. But by starting Climate Change is Elementary and the companion call-to-action program, Two Years to Change, Finnigan aims to make kids the solution. He says, "It's their planet. We borrowed it, but have done a bad job of caring for it." But eight, nine, and ten-year-olds can make change—good change—happen.

With solid teaching methods, good curriculum, and excellent feedback from teachers, parents, and students, Finnigan is planning to expand the program nationally.

This is a sampling of the thousands of entrepreneurial categories that have resulted from the green paradigm shift. Emerging from a prolonged economic downturn, we know that many talent executives will start their own businesses. And many of those who go green will benefit from an increasingly green marketplace.

Green entrepreneurs seed green corporate cultures; anyone joining a green entrepreneurial company will enjoy immediate benefits.

# Conclusion:
## Properly Attired, Our Best Days Lie Ahead!

It is very clear to me that the green paradigm shift will create business executive career opportunities that none of us could ever have imagined five years ago. Properly attired as The Green Suit, each of us will help transform companies and organizations by extending returns on investment and making business a positive force for people and planet. And while it won't happen universally, public opinion of business will become more favorable as companies turn green and become socially responsible.

Adversity and opportunity do go hand in hand. On December 7, 1941, when its fleet at Pearl Harbor suffered a devastating attack by the Japanese empire, the U.S. Navy was left in tatters. Worse, the U.S. Army was small, under-equipped, poorly funded, and ranked eleventh in size (behind Argentina). Newsreels of the day show enlisted men training with what could best be described as toy rifles.

But within months of the start of World War II, the U.S. responded with singular focus and unprecedented funding, sheer grit, and determination, and it used the heavy infusion of monetary and human capital to meet the war head on. In 1942-43, the U.S. armed forces scored impressive land and sea victories at The Battle of Midway and Guadalcanal. Less than four years after the attack on Pearl Harbor, with the end of World War II, the U.S. emerged the world's undisputed military super power.

How did the U.S. transform itself so quickly from military laughingstock to marvel of the world? It could be argued that billions in funding, state-of-the-art weaponry, radar and spy technology, materiel, reliable transport craft, brilliant strategy, and millions of conscripts used to overcome hated adversaries led to this most dramatic of transformations. Since 1945, the U.S. has never lost its military—or for that matter global business—preeminence.

Could the confluence of events affecting global warming and how we acquire and use energy resources lead to a similar transformation? I think so.

After the 1970s, the U.S. relinquished its leadership in renewable energy and other green technologies. And now, thirty years later, as New York Times columnist Thomas Friedman warns, China is poised to "clean our clock on E.T."

It is apparent on several fronts that U.S. businesses are beginning to take these matters seriously; they are becoming better informed of our energy crisis and more familiar with global warming and other irreversible climate-related threats. And many companies are reengineering operations to acquire energy through alternate means such as wind, solar, geothermal, and tidal. They are also using that energy more efficiently by employing smart-grid technology and reducing corporate impact on the environment and society.

But in order to capitalize on this huge transformation—this green paradigm shift—U.S. businesses will need executive talent well-trained and well-informed about sustainability and corporate social responsibility to lead the way.

In 1970, economist Milton Friedman argued that the corporate executive had but one mission: to increase profits for the company and the shareholder. Yet now, the triple bottom line (maximizing profits while running operations in a sustainable fashion and assuring societal benefit) is fast becoming an acceptable practice for business executives.

The company man, the self-reliant executive who sacrificed personal needs and desires for the benefit of his corporation, is gone. In his place are men and women representing a new breed of collaborators—many from the Millennial Generation—who favor all sorts of team dynamics to expand sustainable practices and corporate social responsibility. This cohort is leading us to a new American Dream which is about doing well (achieving career success, owning a home, acquiring wealth, etc.) while doing right (being the good corporate citizen and healing the world). As a result, what and how we think about work and where we work, via the advent of telecommuting, will certainly change, and for the better.

The old model for running company operations often meant top-down management where the C-level dictated requirements and the levels below executed plans to fulfill those requirements. But the new way, as evidenced at companies like CA, balances bottom-up problem-solving and ideation with top-down management goals. CA's Chief Sustainability Officer Steve Boston suffers no lack of well thought out plans, received from CA associates around the globe, to make the company more sustainable and proactive while assuring continued ROI advancement; at CA, company associates see themselves as an essential part of the solution.

In the 1990s, we ushered in the Internet Age and with it a Wild West mindset to create "killer apps" worth billions. The Internet Age was all about money, and some say it was a house of cards that boomed, quickly busted, and contributed to the economic recession of 2000-01. By contrast, being a green business executive is not just about money. It is the realization that The Green Suit can help mitigate daunting climate and energy crises and as a result save the planet.

Personal computing and mobile technology have taken hold of our lives, and the energy required to power such devices has expanded exponentially. Those of us who have gone digital, ditched the daily newspaper, stopped mailing letters in favor of e-mail, have begun participating in social communities, and entered worlds of virtual reality, may have cut substantially our need for products made from wood fiber, but our new online lifestyles have stretched an already overloaded national electrical grid well beyond its tolerances. As coal-fired plants provide most of the U.S.'s power load, it could be argued that the Internet Age rendered us less green.

Surely, politics will continue to play a big role in the growing green economy and creating green jobs. But as evidenced by the increasing number of member resignations from the U.S. Chamber of Commerce, more and more corporations are accepting that they do have a responsibility to mitigate climate change and be good corporate stewards ushering in an age of sustainability and corporate social responsibility.

This new green economy is no flash in the pan. It will define us for generations to come.

The Green Suit is the linchpin for our economic future; these men and women will replace entropy with growth and prosperity. They will also transform the world and in doing so will make green business executive careerism a force of good (and not just profit). And there will be a lot of us in the U.S.: based on my own estimates, The Green Suits universe could top sixty-eight million business executives.

Properly attired as The Green Suit, our best days lie ahead.

The Green Suit is about change and innovation. This business executive is far more than creating renewable energy or green technology; he or she is about making companies run more efficiently and with the least amount of impact on the environment. Surely, the men and women who join the green business executive ranks will play a big role in bringing to market tomorrow's dazzling technological advancements such as: wind turbines for offshore use that resist oxidation (rust buildup); water purification and reclamation systems for drought-stricken areas in Africa that help curb soil erosion and eliminate famine; and smart-grid technology that makes electric power more efficient and affordable.

But more important, they will be about empowering others: many of us will find great personal satisfaction when we extend our career-related talents, teaching at-risk kids to make better choices and avoid lives of crime and violence, and providing the homeless the tools they need to become skilled labor and thrive.

Tailoring the Green Suit is about form and function, empowering yourself for the green career of your dreams. But it is also about process and detail. For many years to come the information we acquire, the knowledge we develop, and the on-the-job skills we hone must never stop. We are all part of the narrative, the unfolding story about the transformation of the world and its economies for a better, more sustainable future.

As you finish reading this book, some of you may react by saying: well this is great, but why didn't he delve into this or explain that? With green business changing daily, poised to grow larger by the day, it would be impossible for me to cover everything; the resulting book would be the size of New York City telephone directory. Even if it detailed every aspect and nuance of green business executive career development, by the time the book reached store shelves it would be out of date (just like that New York City telephone directory).

My biggest goal in writing this book was to guide the process of developing your green business executive career. I want to provide you the structure you need to familiarize yourself with the green business space and help you stay informed of the latest developments, gain awareness of the regulatory landscape, and address environmental concerns that have yet to be imagined.

I was a toddler when my parents took my brothers and me to the 1964 World's Fair in Flushing, New York, much too young to remember the dazzling future that sponsoring companies like IBM, General Motors, and the Walt Disney Company portrayed at their pavilions. Perhaps many of the parents attending scoffed at their kids' wonderment of it all: a vision of pure fantasy. But now it is quite apparent that some of those fantastic, gleaming, futuristic visions are about to become reality. And we, The Green Suits, are going to help make them happen. *Sweet!*

Still, there is plenty to worry us all. While the Millennials are poised to be the driving force of the green paradigm shift, we don't know much about their successors, the Generation Z kids born between 1994 and 2009. How will a cohort so connected to technology and mesmerized by virtual reality relate to their planet in crisis? Will Gen Z kids avert their eyes from the screens of their handheld devices long enough to engage with each other, and the earth?

Earlier, Dave Finnigan pointed to one disturbing reality, that today's elementary school-aged kids are not being exposed to classroom science instruction the way their parents had been thirty and forty years before. Most public schools are mandated by No Child Left Behind and state-level education standards which force time-strapped teachers to "teach to the (assessment) test." Research suggests that typical elementary-aged students are "sponges" for learning, and yet today there are fewer opportunities for them and their classmates to engage in scientific exploration, and for that matter, critical thinking. Add to that, elementary school-aged kids possess limited knowledge of environmental science. And what some kids believe may be the result of misinformation. So Finnigan allocates a good portion of his Climate Change is Elementary program to dealing with the misinformation.

We owe Generation Z and the cohorts to follow the education they need to be better informed, make better life decisions, and seize tomorrow's green career opportunities.

There is so much we don't know about climate change, sustainability, and corporate socially responsible best practices. And that is why every Green Suit must remain well-read, knowledgeable, and continually engaged. We must maintain that fire-in-the-belly enthusiasm and self-assurance that got our nation out of the Great Depression, through World War II, and transformed the U.S. economy into the marvel of the world. As witnesses of—and participants in—the green paradigm shift, we will write this narrative.

But this I do know: our very best days—our shining moments—lie ahead. The work we do as green business executives will usher in an age when business can and will be the agent of change—still focused on ROI, but tasked with using the planet's resources more wisely, achieving sustainability, and making corporate social responsibility the norm and not the exception.

Now is the time to ask—are you ready to begin your executive career in the new green economy?

*Are you ready to tailor your Green Suit?*

# Bibliography

8x8, Inc. http://8x8.com/ (accessed November 15, 2009)

AT&T Intellectual Property. "Strengthening Communities: AT&T Cares." http://www.att.com/gen/corporate-citizenship?pid=7737 (accessed October 15, 2009).

Aker, John. "Level III Fast Charging." *Virginia Summit on Energy Opportunities.* Hampton University, Hampton, Virginia, July 10, 2009.

Alternate Energy Sources. "The Kyoto Protocol Summary: A Quick Guide to Understanding It." http://www.alternate-energy-sources.com/Kyoto-Protocol-summary.html (accessed August 4, 2009).

American Recovery and Reinvestment Act of 2009, The. http://www.opencongress.org/bill/111-s1/show (accessed September 1, 2009).

Ammer, Christine. "Company man," *The American Heritage® Dictionary of Idioms.* New York: Houghton Mifflin, 1997

Babson Executive Education. "About Us." http://execed.babson.edu/info/about.aspx (accessed October 15, 2009).

Baby Boomer Care. "Generation Z Characteristics" http://www.babyboomercaretaker.com/baby-boomer/generation-z/Generation-Z-Characteristics.html (accessed December 1, 2009).

Baker, Mallen. "Corporate Social Responsibility." http://mallenbaker.com/ (accessed August 4, 2009.)

Bard, Mitchell. "The Yom Kippur War." Jewish Virtual Library, Division of the American-Israeli Cooperative Enterprise, 2009. http://www.jewishvirtuallibrary.org/jsource/History/73_War.html (accessed August 4, 2009).

Beard, Randall. Randall Beard's Blog. http://randallbeard.wordpress.com/ (accessed November 14, 2009).

Bennett, Neysa. Telephone interview. January 27, 2010.

Bordman, Gerald and Thomas S. Hischak. "Dreamgirls." *The Oxford Companion to American Theatre*. Oxford: Oxford University Press. 2004.

Boston, Steve. Telephone interview, October 8, 2009.

Boudreau, Joe. Telephone interview, October 15, 2009.

Broughton, Edward. "The Bhopal disaster and its aftermath: a review." *Environmental Health*, May 10, 2005. http://www.ncbi.nlm.nih.gov/pmc/articles/PMC1142333/ (accessed October 10, 2009).

Burrough, Bryan and John Helyar. *Barbarians at the Gate: The Fall of RJR Nabisco*. New York: Harper & Row, 1990.

CO2 IS GREEN. http://co2isgreen.org (accessed November 25, 2009).

C-SPAN. Televised Coverage of the 2008 Democratic National Convention (Denver, Colorado), August 25-28, 2008.

C-SPAN, Televised Coverage of the 2008 Republican National Convention (St. Paul, Minnesota), September 1-4, 2008.

Carson, Rachel. *Silent Spring.* New York: Houghton Mifflin, 1962.

Casual Friday.Dictionary.com. *Dictionary.com's 21st Century Lexicon.* Dictionary.com, LLC. http://dictionary.reference.com/browse/casual Friday (accessed: January 20, 2010).

Clark, Andrew. "US firms quit Chamber of Commerce over climate change position." *Guardian* http://www.guardian.co.uk/business/2009/sep/29/us-chamber-commerce-climate-change September 25, 2009.

Clark, Tony. "White House Solar Panel Goes on Display at Carter Library: 1979 Effort to Encourage Alternative Energy Usage Became 'Road Not Taken'." Jimmy Carter Library & Museum (news release), March 27, 2007.

ClearLead. "Automobile Models: Ford, Honda, Saturn—Jaguar Automobile; Brief overview and history of popular automobile models like Ford, Daimler Chrysler, Jaguar, Lexus and Lincoln." http://www.clearleadinc.com/site/makesandmodels.html (accessed August 5, 2009).

ClimateCounts.org. "What We Believe." http://www.climatecounts.org/about.php (accessed January 20, 2010).

Continental Clothing Company. "EarthPositive® Apparel." http://www.continentalclothing.com/page/about_earthpositive_apparel (accessed January 20, 2010).

Crawford, Tracy. Telephone interview. August 24, 2009.

Crumbock, Lyn. "Recycling, Waste Management and Climate Change." PowerPoint presentation. Cape May County Municipal Utilities Authority, 2009

Davis, Brad. Telephone interview. September 10, 2009.

Deans, Juliana. Telephone interview. October 3, 2009.

Deans, Juliana, L. Firestone and D. Nelson. "Skills-Based Volunteering: Simplified." PowerPoint presentation. *2009 National Conference on Volunteering & Service*, June 22, 2009.

Dennen, Rusty. "Trash Imports Growing Again: More out-of-state trash piling up in Virginia landfills." *Free Lance-Star*, June 15, 2007.

Direct Marketing Association of Washington. *Marketing AdVents*, 2008.

Dominican University of California. "What is The Green MBA®?" http://www.greenmba.com/ (accessed October 28, 2009).

Drucker, Peter F. *The Practice of Management*. New York: Harper Collins, 1954

Eilperin, Juliet. "Scientist steps down during e-mail probe; Hacked messages about global warming caused controversy." *Washington Post*, December 2, 2009. http://www.washingtonpost.com/wp-dyn/content/article/2009/12/01/AR2009120104461.html (accessed December 2, 2009).

Elkington, John. *Cannibals with Forks: Triple Bottom Line of 21st Century Business*. Oxford: Capstone Publishing Ltd., 1999.

Finding Dulcinea: Librarian of the Internet. "On This Day: New York Becomes First Big City to Establish "Pooper Scooper" Law" August 1, 2009. http://www.findingdulcinea.com/news/on-this-day/July-August-08/On-this-Day--New-York-Establishes-Country-s-First--Pooper-Scooper--Law.html (accessed December 8, 2009).

Finnigan, Dave. Telephone interview. November 2, 2009.

Free Encyclopedia of Ecommerce. "Fedex Corp – Early History." http://ecommerce.hostip.info/pages/443/Fedex-Corp-EARLY-HISTORY.html (accessed August 5, 2009).

Friedman, Milton. "The Social Responsibility of Business is to Increase its Profits," *New York Times Magazine*, September 13, 1970. http://www.colorado.edu/studentgroups/libertarians/issues/friedman-soc-resp-business.html (accessed August 5, 2009).

Friedman, Thomas L. "Can I Clean Your Clock?" *New York Times*, July 4, 2009. (Accessed August 3, 2009).

Goleman, Daniel. "Winning in the Age of Radical Transparency." *Harvard Business Review*, May 7, 2009. blogs.hbr.org/leadinggreen/2009/05/radical-transparency.html (accessed August 4, 2009).

Goodman, Ellen. *Close to Home*. New York: Simon & Schuster, 1979.

Goodman, Peter S. "Rising energy prices inflate costs of suburbia and beyond," *New York Times*, June 25, 2008. http://www.nytimes.com/2008/06/25/business/worldbusiness/25iht-exurbs.1.13973643.html (accessed August 4, 2009).

Gotta Mentor. "7 Elements of a Good Story." May 15, 2009. http://www.gottamentor.com/ViewDocument.aspx?d=639 (accessed January 20, 2010).

Gotta Mentor. "What is an Elevator Pitch and Why is it Important?" October 20, 2009. http://www.gottamentor.com/ViewAdvice.aspx?a=322 (accessed January 20, 2010).

Grossman, Ben. Telephone interview. October 4, 2009.

Grossman Marketing. "Green Marketing Solutions." http://grossmanmarketing.com/ServicesSolutions/ServiceSolutionsDetail.asp?ServiceID=17 (accessed November 6, 2009).

Hacker Group. "Hacker Group: Green Philosophy" http://hackergroup.com/index.asp (accessed August 15, 2009).

Hais, Michael D. and Morley Winograd. *Millennial Makeover: MySpace, YouTube, & the Future of American Politics.* Piscataway, N.J.: Rutgers University Press, 2009.

Harris, Lauretta. Telephone interview. September 21, 2009.

Hickman, Leo and James Randerson. "Climate skeptics claim leaked e-mails are evidence of collusion among scientists." *Guardian*, November 20, 2009. http://www.guardian.co.uk/environment/2009/nov/20/climate-sceptics-hackers-leaked-emails (accessed November 21, 2009).

History Place, The. "Pearl Harbor, Hawaii, Sunday, December 7, 1941." http://www.historyplace.com/worldwar2/timeline/pearl.htm (accessed November 17, 2009).

Horsley, Scott and Melissa Block. "Obama Signs Stimulus Bill." *NPR.org*, February 17, 2009. http://www.npr.org/templates/story/story.php?storyId=100785745 (accessed September 1, 2009).

Idea Hive, The. http://theideahive.com/ (accessed December 31, 2009).

Inflationdata.com. "Historical Crude Oil Prices." July 15, 2009. (accessed August 4, 2009).

Inhofe, James M. "Climate Change Update, Senate Floor Statement." January 4, 2005. http://inhofe.senate.gov/pressreleases/climateupdate.htm (accessed September 12, 2009).

Interview Studio. http://interviewstudio.com/Index.do (accessed November 15, 2009).

Ireland, Susan. *The Complete Idiot's Guide to the Perfect Resume, 5th Edition.* New York: Alpha Books, 2010.

Ireland, Susan. Telephone Interview. October 21, 2009.

Jones, Van. *The Green Collar Economy: How One Solution Can Fix Our Two Biggest Problems.* New York: HarperOne, 2008.

Kaplun, Alex. "Exelon Leaves U.S. Chamber Over Climate Dispute." *New York Times*, September 28, 2009. http://www.nytimes.com/gwire/2009/09/28/28greenwire-exelon-leaves-us-chamber-over-climate-dispute-74577.html (accessed October 1, 2009).

Katz, Stuart. Telephone interview. October 1, 2009.

Koltun, Rob. "Investing in water." *Family Office Association: Energy Investing Summit.* Greenwich, Connecticut, July 21, 2009.

Kuhn, Thomas S. *The Structure of Scientific Revolutions.* Chicago: University of Chicago Press, 1962.

Levitt, Steven D. "The Global E-mail We've All Been Waiting For." *New York Times Freakonomics: The Hidden Side of Everything*, December 1, 2009. http://freakonomics.blogs.nytimes.com/2009/12/01/the-global-warming-email-weve-all-been-waiting-for/ (accessed December 2, 2009).

Lifesize Communications. http://lifesize.com (accessed December 1, 2009).

Mayfield, Amanda. Telephone interview. November 16, 2009.

Memmott, Mark. "White House 'Green' Advisor Jones, Under Fire from Beck and Others, Resigns." NPR.org, September 6, 2009. http://www.npr.org/blogs/thetwo-way/2009/09/van_jones_glenn_beck_obama_911.html (accessed September 6, 2009).

Milbank, Dana and Justin Blum. "Document Says Oil Chiefs Met With Cheney Task Force." *Washington Post*, November 16, 2005. (accessed August 3, 2009).

Montgomery County, Maryland. "Fiscal Year 2008 Recycling Rate." http://www.montgomerycountymd.gov/swstmpl.asp?url=/content/

dep/solidwaste/reference/recycling_rate/FY08MassBalForWeb.asp (accessed January 20, 2010).

Monty Python's Completely Useless Web site. http://www.intriguing.com/mp/ (accessed November 15, 2009).

Morriss, Andrew P, William T. Bogart, Andrew Dorchak, Roger E. Meiners. "7 Myths About Green Jobs." *University of Illinois College of Law and Economics Working Paper No. LE09-0007*, 2009.

Neteler, Kas. Telephone interview. October 28, 2009.

Nixon, Richard M. "Statement on Signing the Emergency Daylight Saving Time Energy Conservation Act of 1973," December 15, 1973. http://www.presidency.ucsb.edu/ws/index.php?pid=4073 (Accessed August 4, 2009).

Ottman, J. Consulting. http://www.greenmarketing.com/about-us/ (accessed August 30, 2009).

Ottman, Jacquelyn. Telephone interview. March 3, 2008.

Pernick, Ron, and Clint Wilder. Clean Tech Job Trends 2009." October, 2009.

Pew Center on Global Climate Change. "S.C. Johnson Summary." http://www.pewclimate.org/companies_leading_the_way_belc/company_profiles/sc_johnson (accessed November 28, 2009).

Pickens Plan. "The Plan." http://www.pickensplan.com/theplan/ (accessed August 24, 2009).

Pitts, Byron. "Exxon Valdez Oil Spill: 20 Years Later." CBS Evening News, February 2, 2009. http://www.cbsnews.com/stories/2009/02/02/eveningnews/main4769329.shtml (accessed December 1, 2009).

Princeton Review, The. "Green Honor Roll." http://www.princetonreview.com/green-honor-roll.aspx (accessed October 28, 2009).

RTC Relationship Marketing. "Corporate Social Responsibility." http://www.rtcrm.com/benefits/ (accessed October 15, 2009).

Reel, Monte. "Brazil's Road to Energy Independence; Alterative-Fuel Strategy, Rooted in Ethanol from Sugar Cane, Seen as Model." *Washington Post*, August 20, 2006 http://www.washingtonpost.com/wp-dyn/content/article/2006/08/19/AR2006081900842.html (accessed August 5, 2009).

Research Views. "First Wind Moves Office to Boston from Newton, Massachusetts." http://www.researchviews.com/energy/power/wind/NewsReport.aspx?ArticleID=211492&Industry=Wind&Project=AE (accessed January 29, 2010).

Reuters. "The Iraqi Invasion; In Two Arab Capitals, Gunfire and Fear, Victory and Cheers," August 3, 1990. http://www.nytimes.com/1990/08/03/world/the-iraqi-invasion-in-two-arab-capitals-gunfire-and-fear-victory-and-cheers.html?pagewanted=1 (accessed August 4, 1990).

RiskMetrics Group. "Corporate Governance and Climate Change: Consumer and Technology Companies," December, 2008.

Rockbridge Associates. "Green Technology Index," 2008.

Royal Swedish Academy of Sciences, The. "This Year's Economic Prize to an American" Press release, October 14, 1976. http://nobelprize.org/nobel_prizes/economics/laureates/1976/press.html (accessed October 4, 2009).

Sage, Henry J. "America and the British Empire," *Academic American History: A Survey of America's Past*, 2007. http://www.academicamerican.com/colonial/topics/britishempire.htm (accessed November 1, 2009).

SAIC. "Work-Life Balance," http://www.saic.com/about/corporate-responsibility/our-employees/work-life-balance.html (accessed November 30, 2009).

Scovill Manufacturing Company. Live-voice commercial, *WNBC-TV's The Sixth Hour* (news broadcast). 1971.

SolarPower2Day.net. "The history of solar power." http://www.solarpower2day.net/solar-power/history/ (accessed August 5, 2009).

Stassner, Ken and Diane Wood. "The Engaged Organization: Corporate Employee Environmental Education Survey and Case Study Findings," Marc, 2009.

Start It Up. "So, you are starting a new business ..." December 4, 2009. http://startitupllc.com/2009/12/04/so/ (accessed December 4, 2009).

Sturdy Roots Blog. "Deloitte's CEO on 'Getting Your Hands Dirty'." November 17, 2009. http://sturdyroots.com/2009/11/17/deloittes-ceo-on-getting-your-hands-dirty/ (accessed November 17, 2009).

Sturdy Roots Blog. "In the News: Green Teams at Work Help the Environment." October 12, 2008. http://sturdyroots.com/2008/10/12/in-the-news-green-teams-at-work-help-the-environment/ (accessed November 30, 2009).

Sturdy Roots Blog. "Renew Through Green Jobs Act of 2009 Introduced." April 6, 2009. http://sturdyroots.com/2009/04/06/renew-through-green-jobs-act-of-2009-introduced/ (accessed September 5, 2009).

Sturdy Roots Blog. "The Rise of the Chief Green Officer." July 11, 2009. http://sturdyroots.com/2008/07/11/the-rise-of-the-chief-green-officer/ (accessed July 11, 2009).

Subaru of America. "Environmental Policy," http://www.subaru.com/company/environmental-policy.html (accessed August 4, 2009).

Sweet, Cassandra. "Utility Quits U.S. Chamber Over Rift on Climate Bill." *Wall Street Journal*, September 29, 2009. http://online.wsj.com/article/SB125418835062148235.html (accessed September 29, 2009).

Tabachnick, Jane. "Green Jobs Not Just for the Environment Set." June 10, 2009. http://www.environmentalleader.com/2009/06/10/green-jobs-not-just-for-the-environmental-set/ (accessed August 5, 2009).

Tabachnick, Jane. Telephone interview. October 31, 2009.

Tandberg. "Tandberg Total Telepresence." http://www.tandberg.com/ (accessed December 1, 2009).

Today's Facility Manager, "The Top 10 Green Building Trends to Look for in 2010," Today's Facility Manager Facility Blog, January 13, 2010. http://todaysfacilitymanager.com/facilityblog/2010/01/the-top-10-green-building-trends-to-look-for-in-2010.html (accessed January 20, 2010).

Toastmasters International. "Toastmasters: Public Speaking and More." http://www.toastmasters.org/MainMenuCategories/WhyJoin/PublicSpeakingandMore.aspx (accessed November 30, 2009).

Turk+Taylor. http://turkandtaylor.com/ (accessed December 5, 2009).

Tuss, Adam. "D.C. area gets relief from pain at the pump." WTOP Radio, August 21, 2008. http://stage-v2.wtopnews.com/?sid=1463887&nid=25 (accessed September 12, 2009).

Upton, John. "S.F. expected to exhaust landfill capacity by 2014." *San Francisco Examiner*, March 27, 2009. http://www.sfexaminer.com/

local/SF-expected-to-exhaust-landfill-capacity-by-2014-41957797. html#ixzz0dutOz5yF (accessed January 20, 2010).

United Nations Environment Programme. "Green Jobs Towards Decent Work in a Sustainable, Low-Carbon World," September, 2008.

U.S. Army. "Guadalcanal." http://www.history.army.mil/ brochures/72-8/72-8.htm (accessed December 6, 2009).

U.S. Census Bureau. "2006 American Community Survey," 2007. http://factfinder.census.gov/home/en/acs_pums_2006.html (accessed December 20, 2008).

U.S. Department of Education. "Executive Summary: No Child Left Behind." http://www2.ed.gov/nclb/overview/intro/execsumm. html (accessed December 21, 2009).

U.S. Department of Energy, and Litos Strategic Communication. "The Smart Grid: An Introduction." U.S. Department of Energy Web site, 2008. http://www.oe.energy.gov/ SmartGridIntroduction.htm (accessed January 20, 2010).

U.S. Department of Energy. "Retail Gasoline Historical Prices." http://www.eia.doe.gov/oil_gas/petroleum/data_publications/ wrgp/mogas_history.html (accessed August 5, 2009).

U.S. Environmental Protection Agency. "EPA History" http://www. epa.gov/history/ (accessed August 5, 2009).

U.S. Navy. "Battle of Midway." http://www.history.navy.mil/faqs/ faq81-1.htm (accessed December 6, 2009).

Vander Broek, Anna. "Six-Figure Green Jobs: These days, you can make green by being green." Forbes.com, October 16, 2008. http://www.forbes.com/2008/10/16/sixfigure-green-jobs-lead-corprespons08-cx_avb_1016jobs.html (accessed August 4, 2009).

VisualCV. VisualCV: About Us/Mission. http://visualcv.com/www/about_us/mission.html (accessed September 2, 2009).

Vy and Elle. "About Us: Who We Are." http://www.vyandelle.com/aboutus.html (accessed September 30, 2009).

Vyas, Abhi. Telephone interview. September 30, 2009.

Wal-Mart Stores, Inc. "2009 Global Sustainability Report," 2009.

Wapedia. "Wiki: 1973 oil crisis." http://wapedia.mobi/en/1973_oil_crisis (accessed August 4, 2009).

Weisser, Stanley and Oliver Stone. *Wall Street* (motion picture), 1987.

Woodward, Bob and Carl Bernstein. *All the President's Men.* New York: Simon & Schuster, 1974.

Workforce Management. "Congress Determines 'Green Job' Definition; Stimulus Seeks to Boost Sector," February 10, 2009. http://www.workforce.com/section/00/article/26/16/79.php (accessed August 4, 2009).

Zak, Adam. "CSO 2.0 is part of lean 'n' green evolution." Lean Directions, December, 2008. http://www.sme.org/cgi-bin/get-newsletter.pl?LEAN&20081208&2 (accessed August 4, 2009).

# Acknowledgments

From the day in late July 2009 when I started writing this book, to the day I finished in early December 2009, the business world has endured a roller-coaster ride of sorts. For instance, there have been fluctuations in the price of crude oil, from approximately thirty-four dollars per barrel in August to over sixty dollars per barrel three months later in November; for the first time in over a year, the Dow Jones Industrials pushed past the psychological ten thousand-point benchmark; and Ford Motor Company reported nearly one billion dollars in third quarter profits, the first time that company has seen black ink on its balance sheet in nearly two years.

Then, in late November, the so-called "climate-gate" story broke.

The fluidity of the news cycle presented this first-time author with some formidable challenges, and I could not have completed the manuscript without the help of the truly exceptional and tapped-in people who generously offered their precious time to be my interview subjects, pointed me to newly available and valuable source material, taught me things I did not know, served as my trusted advisors, and encouraged me to write the best book I could.

For this, I owe a debt of gratitude to the following people: John Aker, Linda Barlow, Randall Beard, Neysa Bennett, Alf Blitzer, Steve Boston, Joe Boudreau, Marc Broklawski, John Casey, Jenna Conner Harris, Tracy Crawford, Brad Davis, Juliana Deans, Joe Feigenbaum, Dave Finnigan, Margie French, Ben Grossman, Steve Grossman, Lauretta Harris, Kandy Hilliard, Susan Ireland, Linda Joy, Hilary Kanter, Josef Katz, David Kerr, Sharon Kozinn, Amy LaMarca, Rabbi Devorah Lynn, Marguerite Manteau-Rao, Samantha Mayfield, Linda Carr Muller, Maria Napoli, Kas Neteler, Jacquie Ottman, Albert C. Pollard, Jr., John Prokop, Steve Ross, Nancy Rathbun Scott, Jane Tabachnick, Abhi Vyas, Ed Weisberg, Matthew Weiss, Michèle Wood, and Jackie Young. I would be remiss if I did not take this opportunity to also thank Lauren Black, Cidella Crenshaw, and Joel Pierson and his team for making my first book publishing experience a phenomenal one, and Kathy Abusow and Jason Metnick of the Sustainable Forestry Initiative for their efforts on my behalf.

And many thanks to my in-laws, Helen Weiss and Bob Hall, for their love and support. Sadly, Bob passed away before this book went to print. He lived to heal the world. And I believe he would have been pleased with the final product.

Thirty-one years ago, Don Maxey, the physical sciences teacher at my high school in the Maryland suburbs of Washington, D.C., asked for my help with what he described as "a very urgent matter." Mr. Maxey had discovered that a mining company was dumping asbestos-laden trap rock into the Potomac River, which happens to be the source of Suburban Maryland's and Washington, D.C.'s drinking water. Alarmed that cancer-causing asbestos may have entered the area's water supply, and learning that I had recently gotten to know our local Congressman Newton Steers, Mr. Maxey urged me to contact our representative and ask for his intervention. I called the congressman's office and he and I were quickly connected. With him on the line, I got right to the matter at hand.

Three days later, Congressman Steers followed up by phone; he said that because I called him, the company would no longer be allowed to dump trap rock into the Potomac. I was a high school senior discovering first-hand that anyone—even a skinny seventeen-year-old kid—could make a difference. My lifelong involvement with environmental and public policy activism owes its start to Mr. Don Maxey's request and Congressman Newton Steers' immediate response.

My business career would not have been as fun or rewarding without the guidance and friendship of the late Howard S. Cogan, assistant professor of communications at Ithaca College's Park School of Communications and the genius behind the brilliant "Ithaca is Gorges" ecotourism marketing campaign (which was launched thirty years before anyone knew what ecotourism was). This avuncular man encouraged thousands of ambitious graduates, including myself, to do well, but also to do right. Howard's spirit accompanied me through this book-writing journey.

Twelve years ago, Victoria James made me an offer I could not refuse: to join her as an executive recruiter. Her brand new executive search firm—a sole proprietorship—had taken off like a rocket and there were more executive placement opportunities to seize than hours in the day. Years before, I worked for Victoria in a sales management role and loved the experience. I jumped at the chance to work with her again. Together, we transformed her boutique operation into one of the fastest-growing executive search firms for direct and interactive marketing professionals. With Torie I learned a lot, but also earned a lot. She nurtured me and helped me acquire the skill and the courage to start my own successful head hunting operation, Dan Smolen Direct Search, LLC.

My across the pond friend Russell White co-owns Premier Consultants, which is one of the most successful executive recruiting firms in the United Kingdom. Because IP telephony allows us to call each other toll-free, Russell and I speak regularly. He has opened my eyes to British and European recruitment practices while I have introduced him to our practices in the U.S. And together we are working on international executive placement opportunities. I cannot thank him enough for his honest input, encouragement, and "bloody good" sense of humor.

Karen Vogel and I are close friends and trusted business associates. She is a hardworking business developer and a supremely talented interactive marketing executive who has helped me expand my familiarity with the latest interactive media and social community best practices. Karen has provided me valuable insight and suggested several of the actionable ideas that are included in this book. And lucky for me, she now lives in the Washington, D.C. area which provides us both opportunities to aid each other's business development efforts. Thank you, Karen, for your friendship and all that you have done for me.

And last, Carlos Del Toro, who has a made-for-Hollywood life story: He was born in Havana, where his father was arrested for defying the Castro regime. During a recess in the show trial that surely would have sent his father to prison, the entire Del Toro family received previously requested forty-eight-hour visas to leave Cuba. After hurriedly packing five suitcases, the Del Toros boarded a plane for the short trip to Miami. Two weeks later they arrived at their destination: a rat-infested tenement building in the dangerous Hell's Kitchen neighborhood of New York City made famous in the movie musical, *West Side Story*.

Young Carlos learned the value of hard work and determination from his parents, who between them worked five jobs and earned enough to move the family to a safe neighborhood in Queens, New York. He excelled in public school, graduated from the U.S. Naval Academy, and served his nation with distinction for twenty-three years as a commissioned officer; Carlos' military experience included combat during Operation Desert Storm.

Carlos and I first met when he decided to run for the Virginia House of Delegates. As a candidate, he raised more in campaign contributions than any first-time challenger before him. And while he didn't win his race, Carlos became a role model: every day, he reminds me that through hard work and persistence, anything is possible. His encouragement—even on days when the book-writing didn't come easily—made me work harder, longer, and smarter. Any success that this book brings me is due in large part to Carlos Del Toro's great example. Thank you, Carlos!

# Index

## Symbols

3M Company 74
7 Elements of a Good Story 87
8x8 52, 83
401k 12
401k plan matching 75

## A

academic 15, 34, 91
accreditation 24, 28, 29, 30, 31, 38, 41, 49
Afghanistan 17, 18
Aker, John 72, 83, 97
Aker Wade 72
Alaska 19, 20
All the President's Men 28, 95
American consumers 4, 15
American Dream 11, 78
American economy 11, 17, 18
American Recovery and Reinvestment Act of 2009 (ARRA) 18
American Telephone & Telegraph (AT&T) 11
American Wind Energy Association 25, 42
Anacostia River 20
Antioch University of New England 29
Applied Materials 9
Arctic National Wildlife Refuge (ANWR) 17
Arizona State University 29

AT&T. *See* American Telephone & Telegraph (AT&T)
AT&T Cares 20, 83
authentic lifestyle 30

## B

Babson College 26, 29
Babson Executive Education 26, 27, 29, 56, 83
Baby Boomer Generation xviii
Baker, Mallen 19, 84
Barbarians at the Gate 12, 84
Barrons 25
Bates College 29
Beard, Randall 45, 84, 97
Bennett Baker Group 43
Bennett, Neysa 43, 84, 97
Bhopal 19, 84
biomass xiv, 18
blog 2, 10, 25, 32, 44, 45, 66, 69, 84, 92, 93
blogger 33, 37, 44
blogging 44, 45
BlueGreen Alliance 2
Bogart, William T. 33, 90
Boston Business Journal 73
Boston, Massachusetts 26, 52, 91
Boston, Steve 7, 28, 55, 79, 84, 97
bottom line xiii, xvii, 3, 7, 19, 30, 51, 53, 57, 69, 74, 78, 86
Boudreau, Joe 26, 27, 29, 84, 97
Brazil 16, 91
Burbank, California 57
Burrough, Bryan 12, 84

Bush, George W. 17, 18
Business Council for Sustainable
	Energy 25
Business Week 26

## C

California Green Jobs Summit 63
candidate 23, 31, 38, 40, 41, 42, 45,
	46, 47, 51, 100, 111
Cap and Trade 27
Cape May, New Jersey xvi, 85
carbon dioxide (CO2) 9, 15, 32
carbon footprint xvi, 3, 7, 8, 21, 27,
	49, 53, 57, 63, 65
carbon offsetting 8
carbon sequestration 41
career xi, xii, xvii, xviii, xix, 7, 13, 21,
	23, 27, 28, 30, 31, 32, 34, 35,
	36, 37, 38, 40, 41, 43, 48, 49,
	50, 57, 61, 62, 69, 71, 77, 78,
	80, 81, 82, 98, 111
CareerBuilder 42
career change 27
CareerEco.com 42
Carson, Rachel 11, 85
Carter, Jimmy 14, 85
Case Western Reserve 33
Casual (attire) Fridays 13
Ceres/Risk Metrics 9
certificate programs 28, 49
Cheney, Dick 17
Chevy Volt 72
Chief Executive Officer (CEO) xv, 26,
	34, 60, 72, 76, 92
Chief Financial Officer (CFO) 9, 26
Chief Marketing Officer (CMO) 45,
	73
Chief Sustainability Officer 6, 7, 21,
	79
China 16, 78
chronological résumé 38
Chrysler 9, 85
Chuck the Cup 56
Cisco Systems xiv

City of New York xvi
Clean Tech Job Trends 2009 23, 90
climate change 8, 9, 25, 32, 33, 76,
	79, 82, 85, 88, 90, 91
Climate Change is Elementary 76, 82
climate change skeptics 33, 69
ClimateCounts.org xv, 85
climate gate 33
climatologists 8, 15, 33
cloak-and-dagger 55
CNBC 25
CO2 Is Green 32, 84
CO2 production 15
coal 11, 15, 17, 79
Coca-Cola 9, 10
College of William & Mary 66
communication skill 60
community colleges 31
compact fluorescent lights (CFLs) xvi
company man 11, 12, 73, 78, 83
Complete Idiot's Guide to the Perfect
	Résumé 37
Computer Associates (CA) 7
conservation xiii, xvii, xviii, xix, 3, 8,
	14, 15, 17, 18, 31, 37, 46, 90
consumption 2, 14, 30, 67
Continental Clothing xv, 85
corporate xi, xii, xiii, xiv, xvii, xviii, 2,
	3, 4, 6, 7, 9, 11, 12, 18, 19, 21,
	23, 24, 26, 27, 28, 29, 36, 40,
	41, 43, 51, 52, 53, 54, 55, 56,
	57, 59, 60, 62, 63, 69, 71, 74,
	76, 78, 79, 82, 83, 84, 91, 92
corporate social responsibility (CSR)
	xi, xiii, xiv, xvii, xviii, 2, 3, 4, 7,
	18, 19, 20, 21, 29, 45, 46, 48,
	51, 53, 54, 55, 56, 57, 59, 69,
	71, 78, 79, 82, 84, 91
Crawford, Tracy 2, 23, 85, 97
crude oil xvii, 13, 14, 16, 19, 32, 88,
	97
CSO 7, 95
C-Suite 24, 26, 27, 54
CVWrite.co.uk 41

## D

Datsun 14
Davis, Brad 73, 74, 85, 97
Daylight Savings Time 14
Deans, Juliana 20, 85, 86, 97
degree programs 24, 29, 31
Dell 9
Deloitte 20, 53, 92
Democratic National Convention 17, 84
deniers 32, 33
Denver, Colorado 17, 29, 84
dioxin 11
Direct Marketing Association of Washington 62, 86
discipline-weighted problem solving 28
Dominican University of California 29, 30, 74, 86
Donohue, Tom 33
Dorchak, Andrew 33, 90
Dow Chemical xiv
Dreamgirls xix, 84
DuPont 11, 19

## E

earth positive xv
eBay 57
Ecomagination xiv
economics xviii, 28
ecosystems 2, 15, 53
education xi, xix, 3, 18, 23, 24, 26, 27, 28, 29, 30, 31, 32, 35, 37, 39, 40, 54, 64, 81, 82
Efficient Windows Collaborative 25
Egypt 13
electric vehicle (EV) 72
electric vehicle (EV) fast-charging 72
elevator pitch 59, 60, 61, 62, 67, 87
Elkington, John xiii, 86
Elm City Communications xii, 63
eMeter 57
employee xv, 13, 20, 23, 49, 52, 53, 57, 62, 75, 92

empower 20, 21, 36, 44, 54, 61, 74
empowerment 1, 54, 111
empower staff 54
energy efficiency 8, 48, 52
EnergyStar 68
Engaged Organization 23, 92
Enron 26
environment xiv, xv, 1, 2, 6, 10, 19, 21, 23, 46, 65, 78, 80, 88, 92, 93, 94
environmental xiii, xviii, 2, 3, 6, 7, 8, 10, 11, 15, 23, 26, 29, 51, 56, 63, 81, 84, 92, 93, 94, 98, 111
environmental attorneys 7
environmental engineers 7
EnvironmentalLeader.com 2, 93
environmental meteorologists 8
environmental officer 6
environmental policy 6, 29, 93, 111
Environmental Protection Agency (EPA) 11, 94
environmental science 29, 81
environmental specialists 8
ethanol 16, 91
European Union 41
evangelist 7, 51
executive recruiting xii, 38, 99
executive search 99, 111
executive training 24, 26
Exelon 33, 34, 89
expertise 26, 43, 60, 61, 62, 76
Exxon Valdez 19, 90

## F

Fastcompany.com 8
fax machines 13
Federal Express (FedEx) 13
federal law xvi, 14
file-sharing 21
Financial Times of London 25
Finnigan, Dave 76, 81, 82, 86, 97
First Wind xv, 52, 91
flat-earthers 32
Ford, Gerald R. 14

foreign oil xiv, 14, 15, 17
forestry 3, 8, 25, 98
Fortune 500 xiv, 49
Foster, David 2
France 16
Freakonomics 33, 89
Fredericksburg, Virginia 62
Freegard, Nicola 75
Free Lance-Star 62, 86
Friedman, Milton 12, 18, 19, 78, 87
Friedman, Thomas 16, 78, 87
fuel economy 15
fuel-efficient 14, 16, 57
functional résumé 38

# G

gasoline 13, 16, 94
Gauntlett, Dexter 23
General Electric (GE) xiv, 11
General Motors (GM) 9, 11, 81
Generation Y xvii, xviii
Generation Z xii, 81, 82, 83
George Washington University 29
Georgia Tech 29
geothermal xiv, 8, 18, 25, 78
Geothermal Energy Association 25
Germany 16
global community 57
global warming xiii, xv, 4, 15, 32, 34, 78, 86
goal attainment 49
Goodman, Ellen 11, 87
Gordon Gecko (character) 12
GottaMentor.com 59
government-financial oversight 27
Great Depression 82
green building 3, 93
green business xi, xii, xvii, xviii, xix, 1, 2, 3, 4, 5, 6, 7, 8, 9, 23, 24, 25, 26, 27, 28, 30, 31, 32, 34, 35, 36, 37, 41, 42, 43, 44, 45, 48, 49, 50, 55, 56, 59, 60, 61, 62, 63, 64, 66, 69, 71, 72, 73, 74, 79, 80, 81, 82, 111

green business executive xi, xii, xviii, xix, 1, 2, 3, 4, 5, 6, 7, 8, 9, 23, 24, 28, 31, 32, 35, 36, 37, 41, 42, 43, 48, 49, 50, 55, 59, 61, 63, 64, 66, 69, 79, 80, 81, 82, 111
Green Business Executive Universe 3, 4
GreenCareerCentral.com 42
green collar jobs xvii
green economy xi, xvii, xviii, xix, 17, 26, 32, 34, 46, 51, 79, 80, 82
green fuel 16
Green is Universal xiv
green job, definition 1, 2
green jobs xvii, 1, 2, 3, 9, 10, 17, 18, 23, 26, 31, 32, 33, 63, 64, 66, 79, 90, 92, 93, 94
GreenJobs.BrightGreenTalent.com 42
green jobs czar 1, 18
Green Jobs Myths 33
green marketing 2, 45, 73, 74
Green Marketing 87
Green MBA 30, 74, 86
Green Motivated 4
Green Mountain College 29
green paradigm shift xiii, xiv, 8, 18, 19, 27, 29, 69, 76, 77, 78, 81, 82
Green Practicing 4
GreenProfs.com 42
Green Suit xvii, xviii, xix, xx, 2, 9, 21, 24, 29, 31, 36, 42, 45, 46, 47, 48, 51, 55, 56, 57, 59, 61, 62, 63, 64, 65, 66, 69, 77, 79, 80, 81, 82, 111
greenwashing xiv
Grossman, Ben 72, 73, 87, 97
Grossman Marketing Group 65, 73
Guardian newspaper 33
Gulf War 15

# H

Habitat for Humanity 53

Hacker Group  20, 52, 87
Hais, Mike  xviii, 88
Hampton University  66, 83
Harris, Lauretta  44, 45, 88, 97
Harvard University  29
Hawaii  20, 88
health coverage  75
heating ventilation and cooling (HVAC)  52
Helyar, John  12, 84
hiring manager  23, 31, 35, 36, 37, 38, 42, 43, 45, 46, 47, 48, 54, 61, 64
Honda  9, 14, 85
HotJobs!  42
HSBC  74
Hudson River  11
human capital  xviii, 12, 77
Hummer  16
Hussein, Saddam  15
hybrid  9, 52, 65

## I

IBM  xiv, 7, 9, 74, 81
Inconvenient Truth, The  32
industry  xi, xiv, xix, 1, 15, 20, 30, 59, 60, 61, 65, 66, 74
Inflationdata.com  16, 88
Inhofe, James  32, 88
inner-city  53
Intel  9
Internet  20, 25, 29, 53, 65, 79, 86
interview  xi, 17, 36, 45, 46, 47, 51, 66, 84, 85, 86, 87, 88, 89, 90, 93, 95, 97, 112
InterviewStudio.com  46
Iraq  15, 17, 18
Ireland, Susan  37, 38, 42, 88, 97
Israeli  13, 84

## J

job candidate  23, 31
job-hunting  45
job hunting experience  41, 42

jobs  xvii, 1, 2, 3, 6, 7, 8, 9, 10, 17, 18, 21, 23, 26, 30, 31, 32, 33, 42, 43, 45, 48, 63, 64, 66, 79, 90, 92, 93, 94, 100
Jobs.GreenBiz.com  42
Johnson & Johnson  9
Jones, Van  1, 18, 89
J. Ottman Consulting  74

## K

Katz, Stuart  xii, 63, 89
key words  25, 37, 40, 41
kilowatt hours  68
King George, Virginia  xvi
knowledge  xii, xviii, xix, 16, 23, 24, 26, 27, 28, 29, 34, 36, 41, 45, 56, 59, 74, 80, 81
Koch, Ed  68
Kohlberg Kravis Roberts  12
Kyoto  15, 16
Kyoto Protocol  15, 83

## L

landfill capacity  xvi, 10, 93
Leadership in Energy and Design (LEED)  8
Levitt, Steven D.  33, 89
life cycle assessments  xv
Lifesize Communications  46, 52, 89

## M

Management by Objective (MBO)  13
Marketing AdVents  62, 86
Maryland  xvi, 29, 89, 98
Massachusetts Envelope  73
mass transit commuting  3, 52
Masters of Business Administration (MBA)  29, 30, 38, 74
Mayfield, Samantha CPS  75, 97
Meiners, Roger E.  33, 90
mercantile  11
metrics  37
MetroMedia Technologies  10, 75
Microsoft  52, 75

Microsoft Excel 75
Microsoft PowerPoint 75, 85, 86
Millennial Makeover xviii, 88
Millennials xvii, xviii, 63, 81
Monster 42
Montgomery County, Maryland xvi, 89
Monty Python's Flying Circus 67, 90
Morris, Mark 74
Morriss, Andrew P. 33, 90
Mothlove 75
myths 32, 33, 51, 90

## N

National Retail Federation 73
New York Times 11, 16, 18, 25, 33, 63, 78, 87, 89
New York Times Green Inc. Blog 25
New York Times Magazine. *See* New York Times
Nike 9, 74
Nissan 14
Nixon, Richard M. 11, 14, 90
Nobel Economics Prize 19
No Child Left Behind 81, 94
Northern Virginia xvi, 16, 17, 111
NPR.org 18, 88, 89
nuclear power 15

## O

Obama, Barack 18, 32, 88, 111
online webinars 27
operational costs 57
Organic Trade Association 25
Organization of Petroleum Producing Countries (OPEC) 13, 14, 16
Ottman, Jacquelyn 74, 90
out-of-pocket expense 28
oversight 7, 26, 27, 56

## P

Pacific Rim 15, 41
paradigm shift xiii, xiv, 8, 18, 19, 27, 69, 76, 77, 78, 81, 82

partial zero emission vehicle (PZEV) 52, 65
Pearl Harbor 77, 88
Pedigree 60
People, Planet, Profit xiii
People's Republic of China 16
perchloroethylene (perc) 64
Pernick, Ron 23, 90
PG&E 33
Philadelphia xvi
philanthropy 20
photovoltaic cells 14
Pickens Plan xiv, 90
Pickens, T. Boone xiv, 71
polar ice caps 15
political action committees (501c) 32
politics 32, 79, 88
power management software 53
Presidio School of Management 29
Princeton Review 29, 91
Prince William Sound 19
problem solving 28
problem-solving skill 60

## R

Randall Beard's Blog 84
Ready-Made Résumés 37
Reagan, Ronald 14
recycled content 65
Redmond, Washington 52
referendum 18
regulation 7, 11, 26, 56
regulatory oversight 56
relevance 60
renewable energy xi, xiii, xiv, xv, xvii, xviii, xix, 3, 4, 8, 14, 15, 16, 17, 18, 23, 29, 31, 32, 45, 51, 52, 66, 73, 78, 80
renewable energy managers 8
renewable energy technology 16
Republican National Convention 17, 84
Republican Party 15, 17

research and development (R&D)  1, 14, 15, 34
Research Triangle, North Carolina  66
results  6, 56
résumé  28, 32, 35, 36, 37, 38, 39, 40, 41, 42, 46
résumé recall exercise  39
retail  xvi, 19, 68, 73
return on investment (ROI)  xvii, 7, 35, 51, 74
risk management  28
RJR Nabisco  12, 84
Rockbridge Associates  4, 91
Rodale  74
Rowe, John W.  34
RTC Relationship Marketing  20, 91
Rust Belt  66

## S

SAIC  xv, 92
Salt Lake City, Utah  57
San Francisco, California  xvi, 20
San Mateo, California  57
Sarbanes-Oxley Act  26
Schmidt, Gavin A.  33
science  29, 33, 81, 111
scientists  8, 15, 33, 34, 88
S.C. Johnson  xv, 90
Scovill Manufacturing  12, 92
Seattle  20, 52
secure file-sharing  21
senior executive  26
September 11, 2001  17
service stations  16
Seton Hall University  63
Silent Spring  11, 85
skill-based volunteering  20, 53
smart grid  xix
social communities  6, 25, 43, 79
social networks  25
Solar Electric Power Association  25, 42
Solar Energy Industries Association  25
solar panels  14

solar power  16, 92
South America  15
Space, Zack  31
Spain  16
sport utility vehicle (SUV)  15
Starleaf Business Services  75
Steele, Michael  17
Steers, Newton Congressman  98
stimulus  88, 95
Stonyfield Farm  xv
St. Paul, Minnesota  17, 84
students  24, 63, 76, 81
Sturdy Roots Blog  92
SturdyRoots.com  32, 111
Subaru of America  9, 93
subsidy programs  52
Sunnyvale, California  57
SUNY Binghamton  29
supply chain  10
sustainability  xi, xiii, xiv, xv, xvii, xviii, 1, 2, 4, 6, 7, 9, 10, 21, 23, 28, 29, 30, 32, 36, 37, 45, 46, 48, 49, 51, 52, 54, 55, 56, 57, 59, 60, 69, 71, 76, 78, 79, 82, 95
sustainability director  6
sustainability manager  6
Sustainable Buildings Industry Council  25
sustainable content  65
Sustainable Forestry Initiative  25, 98
Syria  13

## T

Tabachnick, Jane  2, 93, 97
Tailoring the Green Suit  xi, 80
Tandberg  46, 52, 93
Technical Green, LLC  2
TechnicalGreen.net  42
tele-presence  47, 51
tele-work  xv
Tesco plc  9
TheExaminer.com  62
Thornton, Joe Ph.D.  10

three-floor elevator pitch  59, 61, 62, 67
three-legged table approach  66
Three Ps, The  xiii
tidal energy  16, 25
Toastmasters International  61, 93
Toyota  9, 14
trade association  25
training  xi, xix, 3, 7, 18, 23, 24, 26, 27, 28, 30, 31, 32, 35, 37, 40, 45, 46, 47, 54, 55, 56, 64, 77
transparency  xv, xix, 3, 7, 55, 72, 87
triple bottom line  xiii, xvii, 3, 7, 19, 30, 57, 69, 74, 78, 86
Tulsa, Oklahoma  75
Turk+Taylor  74, 93
Twain, Mark  61
Two Years to Change  76
type A personality  13

## U

United Nations Environment Programme (UNEP)  1, 8, 9, 94
United Way  53
University of Chicago  12, 89
University of Colorado at Denver  29
University of East Anglia  33
University of Illinois  33, 90
University of Maryland at College Park  29
University of Michigan  29
University of Texas-Arlington  33
University of Virginia  66
urban planners  8
U.S. Census Bureau's 2006 American Community Survey  4
U.S. Chamber of Commerce  32, 34, 79
U.S. Congress  11, 17
U.S. Department of Labor  18
U.S. Green Buildings Council  25
U.S. House of Representatives  31
U.S. military  xvi

U.S. Small Business Administration (SBA)  71
U.S. Steel  11

## V

Verdiem  53
video-conferencing  21
video interview  46
Virginia  xii, xvi, 4, 16, 17, 62, 66, 83, 86, 100, 111
Virginia Tech  66
virtual CMO  73
virtual face-to-face interviewing  46
virtual office  xviii, 3, 21, 49, 62, 73, 75
VisualCV  42, 95
volunteer  20, 21, 60
Vy and Elle  10, 21, 75, 95
Vyas, Abhi  10, 21, 95, 97

## W

Walker, Rich  6
Wall Street Journal  25, 33, 93
Wall Street (movie)  12, 95
Wal-Mart  xiv, xvi, 9, 95
Walt Disney Company  81
Washington, D.C.  16, 17, 20, 76, 98, 99, 111
water recovery  8
water recycling and reclamation  xvii
water usage  xv
weatherization  31
Web 2.0  20
Web 3.0  42
webinars  27, 31, 63
White House  1, 14, 17, 18, 85, 89, 111
Wilder, Clint  23, 90
wind turbine  8, 16, 80
Winnie, Trevor  23
Winograd, Morley  xviii, 88
workforce education  18
work history  38, 39
work history problems  38

workplace skills 20
World War II 77, 82
Write Communications 44
writing xii, 37, 41, 42, 45, 46, 62, 63,
    69, 81, 97, 98, 100

# Y

Yahoo! 56, 57
Yom Kippur War 13, 84
York College of Pennsylvania 33
YourCause.com 20

## About the Author

Dan Smolen has enjoyed success in a business career that has included sales, marketing, operations, and client-service assignments with leading marketing agencies and service companies, including: Clarion Marketing & Communications, Barry Blau & Partners, and Donnelley Marketing.

He is also a successful executive recruiter of marketing and other business executive talent. Smolen was vice president of Victoria James Executive Search before founding his own company, Dan Smolen Direct Search, LLC, a five-year-old recruitment firm that places business executive talent in assignments across several market verticals, including: green business, direct and interactive marketing, and consumer insights (market research).

In 2005, he was elected Chairman of the Stafford County (Virginia) Democratic Committee, and was heavily involved in the political activities which led two "pro-green business" candidates, Jim Webb and Mark Warner, to the U.S. Senate and Barack Obama to the White House.

He publishes several blogs, including the well-read SturdyRoots.com. And in 1998, he received a U.S. patent for intellectual property supporting interactive marketing communications.

He is also the founder and managing partner of The Green Suits, LLC, a career development and empowerment community for green business executive talent, on the Web at: www.thegreensuits.com.

Smolen earned a Bachelor of Science degree from the Ithaca College Park School of Communications. He is an experienced speaker, and has appeared on radio, television, online, and in print discussing a range of topics, including smart-growth and environmental policy, and green business executive career development. He lives with his family in the Northern Virginia suburbs of Washington, D.C.

Reader comments and suggestions and requests for speaking engagements, interviews, and other appearances may be forwarded to the author at dan@thegreensuits.com.